THROUGH NATURE TO GOD

Contents: The Mystery of Evil; The Cosmic Roots of
Love and Self Sacrifice; Everlasting Reality of Religion;
and much more!

John Fiske

ISBN 1-56459-579-X

Kessinger Publishing Company
Montana, U.S.A.

TO THE BELOVED AND REVERED MEMORY
OF MY FRIEND

THOMAS HENRY HUXLEY

THIS BOOK IS CONSECRATED

PREFACE

 SINGLE purpose runs throughout this little book, though different aspects of it are treated in the three several parts. The first part, "The Mystery of Evil," written soon after "The Idea of God," was designed to supply some considerations which for the sake of conciseness had been omitted from that book. Its close kinship with the second part, "The Cosmic Roots of Love and Self-Sacrifice," will be at once apparent to the reader.

That second part is, with a few slight changes, the Phi Beta Kappa oration delivered by me at Harvard University, in June, 1895. Its original title was "Ethics in the Cosmic Process," and its form of statement was partly determined by the fact that it was intended as a reply to

Huxley's famous Romanes lecture delivered at the University of Oxford in 1893. Readers of "The Destiny of Man" will observe that I have here repeated a portion of the argument of that book. The detection of the part played by the lengthening of infancy in the genesis of the human race is my own especial contribution to the Doctrine of Evolution, so that I naturally feel somewhat uncertain as to how far that subject is generally understood, and how far a brief allusion to it will suffice. It therefore seemed best to recapitulate the argument while indicating its bearing upon the ethics of the Cosmic Process.

I can never cease to regret that Huxley should have passed away without seeing my argument and giving me the benefit of his comments. The subject is one of a kind which we loved to discuss on quiet Sunday evenings at his fireside in London, many years ago. I have observed on Huxley's part, not only in the Romanes lecture, but also in the charming "Prolegomena," written in 1894, a tendency to use the phrase "cosmic process" in a restricted sense as equivalent to "natural selection;" and doubtless if due allowance were made for that circumstance, the appearance of antagonism between us would be greatly diminished. In our many talks, however, I always felt that, along with abundant general sympathy, there was a discernible difference in mental attitude. Upon the proposition that "the foundation of morality is to . . . give up pretending to believe that for which there is no evidence," we were heartily agreed. But I often found myself more strongly inclined than my dear friend to ask the Tennysonian question : —

"Who forged that other influence,
That heat of inward evidence,
By which he doubts against the sense?"

In the third part of the present little book, "The Everlasting Reality of Religion," my aim is to show that "that other influence," that inward conviction, the craving for a final cause, the theistic assumption, is itself one of the master facts of the universe, and as much entitled to respect as any fact in physical nature can possibly be. The argument flashed upon me about ten years ago, while reading Herbert Spencer's controversy with Frederic Harrison concerning the nature and reality of religion. Because Spencer derived historically the greater part of the modern belief in an Unseen World from the savage's primeval world of dreams and ghosts, some of his critics maintained that logical consistency required him to dismiss the modern belief as utterly false; otherwise he would be guilty of seeking to evolve truth from falsehood. By no means, replied Spencer: "Contrariwise, the ultimate form of the religious consciousness is the final development of a consciousness which at the outset contained a germ of truth obscured by multitudinous errors." This suggestion has borne fruit in the third part of the present volume, where I have introduced a wholly new line of argument to show that

the Doctrine of Evolution, properly understood, does not leave the scales equally
balanced between Materialism and Theism,
but irredeemably discredits the former,
while it places the latter upon a firmer
foundation than it has ever before occupied.

My reference to the French materialism
of the eighteenth century, in its contrast
with the theism of Voltaire, is intended to
point the stronger contrast between the
feeble survivals of that materialism in our
time and the unshakable theism which is in
harmony with the Doctrine of Evolution.
When some naturalist like Haeckel assures
us that as evolutionists we are bound to
believe that death ends all, it is a great
mistake to hold the Doctrine of Evolution
responsible for such a statement. Haeckel's opinion was never reached through a
scientific study of evolution; it is nothing
but an echo from the French speculation
of the eighteenth century. Such a writer
as La Mettrie proceeded upon the assumption that no belief concerning anything in

the heavens above, or the earth beneath,
or the waters under the earth, is worthy
of serious consideration unless it can be
demonstrated by the methods employed in
physical science. Such a mental attitude
was natural enough at a time when the
mediæval theory of the world was falling
into discredit, while astronomy and physics
were winning brilliant victories through the
use of new methods. It was an attitude
likely to endure so long as the old-fashioned
fragmentary and piecemeal habits of study-
ing nature were persisted in ; and the
change did not come until the latter half
of the nineteenth century.

The encyclopædic attainments of Alex-
ander von Humboldt, for example, left him,
to all intents and purposes, a materialist of
the eighteenth century. But shortly before
the death of that great German scholar,
there appeared the English book which her-
alded a complete reversal of the attitude of
science. The " Principles of Psychology,"
published in 1855 by Herbert Spencer, was

the first application of the theory of evolution on a grand scale. Taken in connection
with the discoveries of natural selection, of
spectrum analysis, and of the mechanical
equivalence between molar and molecular
motions, it led the way to that sublime conception of the Unity of Nature by which
the minds of scientific thinkers are now
coming to be dominated. The attitude of
mind which expressed itself in a great encyclopædic book without any pervading principle of unity, like Humboldt's "Kosmos,"
is now become what the Germans call *ein
ueberwundener Standpunkt*, or something
that we have passed by and left behind.

When we have once thoroughly grasped
the monotheistic conception of the universe
as an organic whole, animated by the omnipresent spirit of God, we have forever
taken leave of that materialism to which
the universe was merely an endless multitude of phenomena. We begin to catch
glimpses of the meaning and dramatic purpose of things ; at all events we rest as-

sured that there really is such a meaning. Though the history of our lives, and of all life upon our planet, as written down by the unswerving finger of Nature, may exhibit all events and their final purpose in unmistakable sequence, yet to our limited vision the several fragments of the record, like the leaves of the Cumæan sibyl, caught by the fitful breezes of circumstance and whirled wantonly hither and thither, lie in such intricate confusion that no ingenuity can enable us wholly to decipher the legend. But could we attain to a knowledge commensurate with the reality — could we penetrate the hidden depths where, according to Dante (*Paradiso*, xxxiii. 85), the story of Nature, no longer scattered in truant leaves, is bound with divine love in a mystic volume, we should find therein no traces of hazard or incongruity. From man's origin we gather hints of his destiny, and the study of evolution leads our thoughts through Nature to God.

CAMBRIDGE, March 2, 1899.

CONTENTS

xiv   *Contents*

Contents   xv

THE MYSTERY OF EVIL

I am the Lord, and there is none else. I form the light,
and create darkness; I make peace, and create evil. I the
Lord do all these things. — ISAIAH, xlv. 6, 7.

Did not our God bring all this evil upon us? — NEHEMIAH,
xiii. 18.

Οὐκ ἔοικε δ' ἡ φύσις ἐπεισοδιώδης οὖσα ἐκ τῶν φαινομένων, ὥσπερ
μοχθηρὰ τραγῳδία. — ARISTOTLE, *Metaphysica*, xiii. 3.

I

The Serpent's Promise to the Woman

" Your eyes shall be opened, and ye shall be as gods, knowing good and evil." *Genesis* iii. 5.

HE legend in which the serpent is
represented as giving this counsel
to the mother of mankind occurs
at the beginning of the Pentateuch in the
form which that collection of writings assumed after the return of the Jews from
the captivity at Babylon, and there is good
reason for believing that it was first placed
there at that time. Allusions to Eden in
the Old Testament literature are extremely
scarce,[1] and the story of Eve's temptation
first assumes prominence in the writings
of St. Paul. The marks of Zoroastrian
thought in it have often been pointed out.
This garden of Eden is a true Persian para-

[1] Isaiah li. 3 ; Joel ii. 3 ; Ezekiel xxviii. 13, xxxi. 8, 9.

dise, situated somewhere in that remote wonderland of Aryana Vaëjo to which all Iranian tradition is so fond of pointing back. The wily serpent is a genuine Parsee serpent, and the spirit which animates him is that of the malicious and tricksome Ahriman, who takes delight in going about after the good creator Ormuzd and spoiling his handiwork. He is not yet identified with the terrible Satan, the accusing angel who finds out men's evil thoughts and deeds. He is simply a mischief-maker, and the punishment meted out to him for his mischief reminds one of many a curious passage in the beast epos of primitive peoples. As in the stories which tell why the mole is blind or why the fox has a bushy tail, the serpent's conduct is made to account for some of his peculiar attributes. As a punishment he is made to crawl upon his belly, and be forever an object of especial dread and loathing to all the children of Eve.

What, then, is the crime for which the serpent Ahriman thus makes bitter expia-

tion? In what way has he spoiled Ormuzd's last and most wonderful creation?
He has introduced the sense of sin: the
man and the woman are afraid, and hide
themselves from their Lord whom they
have offended. Yet he has been not alto-
gether a deceiving serpent. In one respect
he had spoken profound truth. The man
and the woman have become as gods. In
the Hebrew story Jehovah says, " Behold
the man is become as one of us ; " that is
to say, one of the Elohim or heavenly host,
who know the good and the evil. Man has
apparently become a creature against whom
precautions need to be taken. It is hinted
that by eating of the other tree and acquiring immortal life he would achieve some
result not in accordance with Jehovah's
will, yet which it would then be too late to
prevent. Accordingly, any such proceed-
ings are forestalled by driving the man and
woman from the garden, and placing senti-
nels there with a fiery sword which turns
hither and thither to warn off all who would

tread the path that leads to the tree of life. The anthropomorphism of the story is as vivid as in those Homeric scenes in which gods and men contend with one another in battle. It is plainly indicated that Jehovah's wrath is kindled at man's presumption in meddling with what belongs only to the Elohim; man is punished for his arrogance in the same spirit as when, later on, he gives his daughters in marriage to the sons of the Elohim and brings on a deluge, or when he strives to build a tower that will reach to heaven and is visited with a confusion of tongues. So here in Eden he has come to know too much, and Ahriman's heinous crime has consisted in helping him to this interdicted knowledge.

The serpent's promise to the woman was worthy of the wisest and most astute of animals. But with yet greater subtlety he might have declared, Except ye acquire the knowledge of good and evil, ye cannot come to be as gods; divine life can never be yours. Throughout the Christian world this legend of the lost paradise has figured as the story of the Fall of Man ; and naturally, because of the theological use of it made by St. Paul, who first lifted the story into prominence in illustrating his theory of Christ as the second Adam : since by man came death into the world, by man came also the resurrection from death and from sin. That there is truth of the most vital sort in the Pauline theory is undeniable ; but there are many things that will bear looking at from opposite points of view, for aspects of truth are often to be found on both sides of the shield, and there is a sense in which we may regard the loss of paradise as in itself the beginning of the Rise of Man. For this, indeed, we have already found some justification in the legend itself. It is in no spirit of paradox that I make this suggestion. The more patiently one scrutinizes the processes whereby things have come to be what they are, the more deeply is one impressed with its profound significance.

II

The Pilgrim's Burden

UT before I can properly elucidate this view, and make clear what is meant by connecting the loss of innocence with the beginning of the Rise of Man, it is necessary to bestow a few words upon a well-worn theme, and recall to mind the helpless and hopeless bewilderment into which all theologies and all philosophies have been thrown by the problem of the existence of evil. From the ancient Greek and Hebrew thinkers who were saddened by the spectacle of wickedness insolent and unpunished, down to the aged Voltaire and the youthful Goethe who felt their theories of God's justice quite baffled by the Lisbon earthquake, or down to the atheistic pessimist of our own time who asserts that the Power which sustains the world is but a blind and terrible force without concern for man's welfare of body or of soul, — from first to last the history of philosophy teems with the mournful instances of this discouragement. In that tale of War and Peace wherein the fervid genius of Tolstoi has depicted scenes and characters of modern life with truthful grandeur like that of the ancient epic poems, when our friend, the genial and thoughtful hero of the story, stands in the public square at Moscow, uncertain of his fate, while the kindly bright-faced peasant and the eager pale young mechanic are shot dead by his side, and all for a silly suspicion on the part of Napoleon's soldiery; as he stands and sees the bodies, still warm and quivering, tossed into a trench and loose earth hastily shovelled over them, his manly heart surges in rebellion against a world in which such things can be, and a voice within him cries out, — not in the mood in which the fool crieth, but with the anguish of a tender soul wrung by the sight

of stupendous iniquity, — " There is no
God ! "   It is but the utterance of an old-
world feeling, natural enough to hard-
pressed and sorely tried humanity in those
moments that have come to it only too
often, when triumphant wrong is dreadfully
real and close at hand, while anything like
compensation seems shadowy and doubtful
and far away.

It is this feeling that has created the
belief in a devil, an adversary to the good
God, an adversary hard to conquer or baffle.
The feeling underlies every theological
creed, and in every system of philosophy
we find it lurking somewhere.   In these
dark regions of thought, which science has
such scanty means for exploring, the statements which make up a creed are apt to
be the outgrowth of such an all-pervading
sentiment, while their form will be found
to vary with the knowledge of nature —
meagre enough at all times, and even in
our boasted time — which happens to char-
acterize the age in which they are made.

Hence, well-nigh universally has philosophy proceeded upon the assumption, whether tacit or avowed, that pain and wrong are things hard to be reconciled with the theory that the world is created and ruled by a Being at once all-powerful and all-benevolent. Why does such a Being permit the misery that we behold encompassing us on every side? When we would fain believe that God is love indeed, and love creation's final law, how comes it that nature, red in tooth and claw with ravine, shrieks against our creed? If this question could be fairly answered, does it not seem as if the burden of life, which so often seems intolerable, would forthwith slip from our shoulders, and leave us, like Bunyan's pilgrim, free and bold and light-hearted to contend against all the ills of the world?

Ever since human intelligence became enlightened enough to grope for a meaning and purpose in human life, this problem of the existence of evil has been the burden of man. In the effort to throw it off, leaders of thought have had recourse to almost every imaginable device. It has usually been found necessary to represent the Creator as finite either in power or in goodness, although the limitation is seldom avowed, except by writers who have a leaning toward atheism and take a grim pleasure in pointing out flaws in the constitution of things. Among modern writers the most conspicuous instance of this temper is afforded by that much too positive philosopher Auguste Comte, who would fain have tipped the earth's axis at a different angle and altered the arrangements of nature in many fanciful ways. He was like Alphonso, the learned king of Castile, who regretted that he had not been present when the world was created, — he could have given such excellent advice!

In a very different mood the great Leibnitz, in his famous theory of optimism, argued that a perfect world is in the nature of things impossible, but that the world in which we live is the best of possible worlds.

The limitation of the Creator's power is made somewhat more explicitly by Plato, who regarded the world as the imperfect realization of a Divine Idea that in itself is perfect. It is owing to the intractableness and vileness of matter that the Divine Idea finds itself so imperfectly realized. Thus the Creator's power is limited by the nature of the material out of which he makes the world. In other words, the world in which we live is the best the Creator could make out of the wretched material at his disposal. This Platonic view is closely akin to that of Leibnitz, but is expressed in such wise as to lend itself more readily to myth-making. Matter is not only considered as what Dr. Martineau would call a "datum objective to God," but it is endowed with a diabolical character of its own.

III

Manichæism and Calvinism

T is but a step from this to the complicated personifications of Gnosticism, with its Demiurgus, or inferior spirit that created the world. By some of the Gnostics the Creator was held to be merely an inferior emanation from God, a notion which had a powerful indirect effect upon the shaping of Christian doctrine in the second and third centuries of our era. A similar thought appears in the mournful question asked by Tennyson's Arthur :—

> "O me! for why is all around us here
> As if some lesser god had made the world
> And had not force to shape it as he would?"

But some Gnostics went so far as to hold that the world was originally created by the Devil, and is to be gradually purified and redeemed by the beneficent power of God as manifested through Jesus Christ. This notion is just the opposite to that of the Vendidad, which represents the world as coming into existence pure and perfect, only to be forthwith defiled by the trail of the serpent Ahriman. In both these opposing theories the divine power is distinctly and avowedly curtailed by the introduction of a rival power that is diabolical ; upon this point Parsee and Gnostic are agreed. Distinct sources are postulated for the evil and the good. The one may be regarded as infinite in goodness, the other as infinite in badness, and the world in which we live is a product of the everlasting conflict between the two. This has been the fundamental idea in all Manichæan systems, and it is needless to say that it has always exerted a mighty influence upon Christian theology. The Christian conception of the Devil, as regards its deeper ethical aspect, has owed much to the Parsee conception of Ahriman. It can hardly be said, however,

that there has been any coherent, closely
reasoned, and generally accepted Christian
theory of the subject. The notions just
mentioned are in themselves too shadowy
and vague, they bear too plainly the marks
of their mythologic pedigree, to admit of
being worked into such a coherent and
closely reasoned theory. Christian thought
has simply played fast and loose with these
conceptions, speaking in one breath of divine omnipotence, and in the next alluding
to the conflict between good and evil in
language fraught with Manichæism.

In recent times Mr. John Stuart Mill
has shown a marked preference for the
Manichæan view, and has stated it with
clearness and consistency, because he is not
hampered by the feeling that he ought to
reach one conclusion rather than another.
Mr. Mill does not urge his view upon the
reader, nor even defend it as his own view,
but simply suggests it as perhaps the view
which is for the theist most free from difficulties and contradictions. Mr. Mill does

not, like the Manichæans, imagine a personified principle of evil; nor does he, like Plato, entertain a horror of what is sometimes, with amusing vehemence, stigmatized as " brute matter." He does not undertake to suggest how or why the divine power is limited; but he distinctly prefers the alternative which sacrifices the attribute of omnipotence in order to preserve in our conception of Deity the attribute of goodness. According to Mr. Mill, we may regard the all-wise and holy Deity as a creative energy that is perpetually at work in eliminating evil from the universe. His wisdom is perfect, his goodness is infinite, but his power is limited by some inexplicable viciousness in the original constitution of things which it must require a long succession of ages to overcome. In such a view Mr. Mill sees much that is ennobling. The humblest human being who resists an impulse to sin, or helps in the slightest degree to leave the world better than he found it, may actually be regarded as a

participator in the creative work of God;
and thus each act of human life acquires a
solemn significance that is almost overwhelming to contemplate.

These suggestions of Mr. Mill are extremely interesting, because he was the last
great modern thinker whose early training
was not influenced by that prodigious expansion of scientific knowledge which, since
the middle of the nineteenth century, has
taken shape in the doctrine of evolution.
This movement began early enough to de-
termine the intellectual careers of eminent
thinkers born between 1820 and 1830, such
as Spencer and Huxley. Mr. Mill was a
dozen years too old for this. He was born
at nearly the same time as Mr. Darwin, but
his mental habits were formed too soon for
him to profit fully by the new movement of
thought; and although his attitude toward
the new ideas was hospitable, they never
fructified in his mind. While his thinking
has been of great value to the world, much
of it belongs to an era which we have now

left far behind. This is illustrated in the
degree to which he was influenced by the
speculations of Auguste Comte. Probably
no two leaders of thought, whose dates of
birth were scarcely a quarter of a century
apart, were ever separated by such·a stupendous gulf as that which intervenes between Auguste Comte and Herbert Spencer, and this fact may serve as an index to
the rapidity of movement which has characterized the nineteenth century. Another
illustration of the old-fashioned character
of Mill's philosophy is to be seen in his use
of Paley's argument from design in support
of the belief in a beneficent Creator. Mill
adopted this argument, and, as a professed
free-thinker, carried it to the logical conclusion from which Paley, as a churchman,
could not but shrink. This was the conclusion which I have already mentioned,
that God's creative power has been limited
by some inexplicable viciousness in the
original constitution of things.

I feel as if one could not be too grateful

to Mr. Mill for having so neatly and sharply stated, in modern language and with modern illustrations, this old conclusion, which after all is substantially that of Plato and the Gnostics. For the shock which such a clear, bold statement gives to our religious feelings is no greater than the shock with which it strikes counter to our modern scientific philosophy. Suppose we could bring back to earth a Calvinist of the seventeenth century and question him. He might well say that the God which Mr. Mill offers us, shorn of the attribute of omnipotence, is no God at all. He would say with the Hebrew prophet, that God has created the evil along with the good, and that he has done so for a purpose which human reason, could it once comprehend all the conditions of the case, would most surely approve as infinitely wise and holy. Our Calvinist would ask who is responsible for the original constitution of things if not the Creator himself, and in supposing anything essentially vicious in that constitution, have not Plato

and the Gnostics and the Manichæans and
Mr. Mill simply taken counsel of their ignorance? Nay, more, the Calvinist would
declare that if we really understood the
universe of which humanity is a part, we
should find scientific justification for that
supreme and victorious faith which cries,
"Though he slay me, yet will I trust in
him!" The man who has acquired such
faith as this is the true freeman of the universe, clad in stoutest coat of mail against
disaster and sophistry, — the man whom
nothing can enslave, and whose guerdon is
the serene happiness that can never be
taken away.

IV

The Dramatic Unity of Nature

OW in these strong assertions it seems to me that the Calvinist is much more nearly in accord with our modern knowledge than are Plato and Mill. It is not wise to hazard statements as to what the future may bring forth, but I do not see how the dualism implied in all these attempts to refer good and evil to different creative sources can ever be seriously maintained again. The advance of modern science carries us irresistibly to what some German philosophers call monism, but I prefer to call it monotheism. In getting rid of the Devil and regarding the universe as the multiform manifestation of a single all-pervading Deity, we become for the first time pure and uncompromising monotheists, — believers in the ever-living, unchangeable, and all-wise Heavenly Father, in whom we may declare our trust without the faintest trace of mental reservation.

If we can truly take such a position, and hold it rationally, it is the modern science so apt to be decried by the bats and owls of orthodoxy that justifies us in doing so. For what is the philosophic purport of these beautiful and sublime discoveries with which the keen insight and patient diligence of modern students of science are beginning to be rewarded? What is the lesson that is taught alike by the correlation of forces, by spectrum analysis, by the revelations of chemistry as to the subtle behaviour of molecules inaccessible to the eye of sense, by the astronomy that is beginning to sketch the physical history of countless suns in the firmament, by the palæontology which is slowly unravelling the wonders of past life upon the earth through millions of ages? What is the grand lesson that is taught by all this? It is the lesson of the unity of nature. To learn it rightly is to learn that all the things that we can see and know, in the course of our life in this world, are so intimately woven together that nothing could be left out without reducing the whole marvellous scheme to chaos. Whatever else may be true, the conviction is brought home to us that in all this endless multifarious-ness there is one single principle at work, that all is tending toward an end that was involved from the very beginning, if one can speak of beginnings and ends where the process is eternal. The whole universe is animated by a single principle of life, and whatever we see in it, whether to our half-trained understanding and narrow experience it may seem to be good or bad, is an indispensable part of the stupendous scheme. As Aristotle said, so long ago, in one of those characteristic flashes of insight into the heart of things in which no one has ever excelled him, in nature there is nothing that is out of place or interpolated, as in an ill-constructed drama.

To-day we can begin to realize how much

was implied in this prophetic hint of Aristotle's, for we are forced to admit that whatever may be the function of evil in this world, it is unquestionably an indispensable function, and not something interpolated from without. Whatever exists is part of the dramatic whole, and this can quickly be proved. The goodness in the world — all that we love and praise and emulate — we are ready enough to admit into our scheme of things, and to rest upon it our belief in God. The misery, the pain, the wickedness, we would fain leave out. But if there were no such thing as evil, how could there be such a thing as goodness? Or to put it somewhat differently, if we had never known anything but goodness, how could we ever distinguish it from evil? How could we recognize it as good? How would its quality of goodness in any wise interest or concern us? This question goes down to the bottom of things, for it appeals to the fundamental conditions according to which conscious intelligence exists at all.

Its answer will therefore be likely to help us. It will not enable us to solve the problem of evil, enshrouded as it is in a mystery impenetrable by finite intelligence, but it will help us to state the problem correctly; and surely this is no small help. In the mere work of purifying our intellectual vision there is that which heals and soothes us. To learn to see things without distortion is to prepare one's self for taking the world in the right mood, and in this we find strength and consolation.

V

What Conscious Life is made of

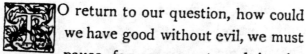

O return to our question, how could we have good without evil, we must pause for a moment and inquire into the constitution of the human mind. What we call the soul, the mind, the conscious self, is something strange and wonderful. In our ordinary efforts to conceive it, invisible and impalpable as it is, we are apt to try so strenuously to divorce it from the notion of substance that it seems ethereal, unreal, ghostlike. Yet of all realities the soul is the most solid, sound, and undeniable. Thoughts and feelings are the fundamental facts from which there is no escaping. Our whole universe, from the sands on the seashore to the flaming suns that throng the Milky Way, is built up of sights and sounds, of tastes and odours, of pleasures and pains, of sensations of motion and resistance either felt directly or inferred. This is no ghostly universe, but all intensely real as it exists in that intensest of realities, the human soul! Consciousness, the soul's fundamental fact, is the most fundamental of facts. But a truly marvellous affair is consciousness! The most general truth that we can assert with regard to it is this, that it exists only by virtue of incessant change. A state of consciousness that should continue through an appreciable interval of time without undergoing change would not be a state of consciousness. It would be unconsciousness.

This perpetual change, then, is what makes conscious life. It is only by virtue of this endless procession of fleeting phases of consciousness that the human soul exists at all. It is thus that we are made. Why we should have been made thus is a question aiming so far beyond our ken that it is idle to ask it. We might as well inquire whether Infinite Power could have made twice two equal five. We must rest content with knowing that it is thus we were created; it is thus that the human soul exists. Just as dynamic astronomy rests upon the law of gravitation, just as physics is based upon the properties of waves, so the modern science of mind has been built upon the fundamental truth that consciousness exists only by virtue of unceasing change. Our conscious life is a stream of varying psychical states which quickly follow one another in a perpetual shimmer, with never an instant of rest. The elementary psychical states, indeed, lie below consciousness, or, as we say, they are sub-conscious. We may call these primitive pulsations the psychical molecules out of which are compounded the feelings and thoughts that well up into the full stream of consciousness. Just as in chemistry we explain the qualitative differences among things as due to diversities of arrangement among compounded molecules and atoms, so in psychology we have come to see that thoughts and feelings in all their endless variety are diversely compounded of sub-conscious psychical molecules.

Musical sounds furnish us with a simple and familiar illustration of this. When the sounds of taps or blows impinge upon the ear slowly, at the rate of not more than sixteen in a second, they are cognized as separate and non-musical noises. When they pass beyond that rate of speed, they are cognized as a continuous musical tone of very low pitch; a state of consciousness which seems simple, but which we now see is really compound. As the speed of the blows increases, further qualitative differences arise; the musical tone rises in pitch until it becomes too acute for the ear to cognize, and thus vanishes from consciousness. But this is far from being the whole story; for the series of blows or pulsations make not only a single vivid fundamental tone, but also a multifarious companion group of fainter overtones, and the diverse blending of these faint harmonics constitutes the whole difference in tone quality between the piano and the flute, the violin and the trumpet, or any other instruments. If you take up a violin and sound the F one octave above the treble staff, there are produced, in the course of a single second, several thousand psychical states which together make up the sensation of pitch, fifty-five times as many psychical states which together make up the sensation of tone quality, and an immense number of other psychical states which together make up the sensation of intensity. These psychical states are not, in any strict sense of the term, states of consciousness; for if they were to rise individually into consciousness, the result would be an immense multitude of sensations, and not a single apparently homogeneous sensation. There is no alternative but to conclude that .in this case a seemingly simple state of consciousness is in reality compounded of an immense multitude of sub-conscious psychical changes.

Now, what is thus true in the case of musical sounds is equally true of all states of consciousness whatever, both those that we call intellectual and those that we call emotional. All are highly compounded aggregates of innumerable minute sub-conscious psychical pulsations, if we may so call them. In every stream of human consciousness that we call a soul each second of time witnesses thousands of infinitely small changes, in which one fleeting group of pulsations in the primordial mind-stuff gives place to another and a different but equally fleeting group. Each group is unlike its immediate predecessor. The absence of difference would be continuance, and continuance means stagnation, blankness, negation, death. That ceaseless flutter, in which the quintescence of conscious life consists, is kept up by the perpetual introduction of the relations of likeness and unlikeness. Each one of the infinitesimal changes is a little act of discrimination, a recognition of a unit of feeling as either like or unlike some other unit of feeling. So in these depths of the soul's life the arrangements and re-arrangements of units go on, while on the surface the results appear from moment to moment in sensations keen or dull, in perceptions clear or vague, in judgments wise or foolish, in memories gay or sad, in sordid or lofty trains of thought, in gusts of anger or thrills of love. The whole fabric of human thought and human emotion is built up out of minute sub-conscious discriminations of likenesses and unlikenesses, just as much as the material world in all its beauty is built up out of undulations among invisible molecules.

VI

Without the Element of Antagonism there could be no Consciousness, and therefore no World

E may now come up out of these depths, accessible only to the plummet of psychologic analysis, and move with somewhat freer gait in the region of common and familiar experiences. It is an undeniable fact that we cannot know anything whatever except as contrasted with something else. The contrast may be bold and sharp, or it may dwindle into a slight discrimination, but it must be there. If the figures on your canvas are indistinguishable from the background, there is surely no picture to be seen. Some element of unlikeness, some germ of antagonism, some chance for discrimination, is essential to every act of knowing. I might

have illustrated this point concretely without all the foregoing explanation, but I
have aimed at paying it the respect due to
its vast importance.   I have wished to show
how the fact that we cannot know anything
whatever except as contrasted with something else is a fact that is deeply rooted in
the innermost structure of the human mind.
It is not a superficial but a fundamental
truth, that if there were no colour but red it
would be exactly the same thing as if there
were no colour at all.   In a world of unqualified redness, our state of mind with regard
to colour would be precisely like our state
of mind in the present world with regard to
the pressure of the atmosphere if we were
always to stay in one place.   We are always
bearing up against the burden of this deep
aerial ocean, nearly fifteen pounds upon
every square inch of our bodies ; but until
we can get a chance to discriminate, as by
climbing a mountain, we are quite unconscious of this heavy pressure.   In the same
way, if we knew but one colour we should

know no colour. If our ears were to be
filled with one monotonous roar of Niagara,
unbroken by alien sounds, the effect upon
consciousness would be absolute silence.
If our palates had never come in contact
with any tasteful thing save sugar, we should
know no more of sweetness than of bitter-
ness. If we had never felt physical pain,
we could not recognize physical pleasure.
For want of the contrasted background its
pleasurableness would be non-existent. And
in just the same way it follows that without
knowing that which is morally evil we could
not possibly recognize that which is morally
good. Of these antagonist correlatives,
the one is unthinkable in the absence of
the other. In a sinless and painless world,
human conduct might possess more outward marks of perfection than any saint
ever dreamed of ; but the moral element
would be lacking ; the goodness would have
no more significance in our conscious life
than that load of atmosphere which we are
always carrying about with us.

We are thus brought to a striking conclusion, the essential soundness of which
cannot be gainsaid. In a happy world there
must be sorrow and pain, and in a moral
world the knowledge of evil is indispensable. The stern necessity for this has been
proved to inhere in the innermost constitution of the human soul. It is part and parcel of the universe. To him who is disposed
to cavil at the world which God has in such
wise created, we may fairly put the question whether the prospect of escape from
its ills would ever induce him to put off this
human consciousness, and accept in ex-
change some form of existence unknown
and inconceivable! The alternative is clear:
on the one hand a world with sin and suffering, on the other hand an unthinkable
world in which conscious life does not in-
volve contrast.

The profound truth of Aristotle's remark
is thus more forcibly than ever brought
home to us. We do not find that evil has
been interpolated into the universe from

without ; we find that, on the contrary, it is an indispensable part of the dramatic whole.   God is the creator of evil, and from the eternal scheme of things diabolism is forever excluded.   Ormuzd and Ahriman have had their day and perished, along with the doctrine of special creations and other fancies of the untutored human mind. From our present standpoint we may fairly ask, What would have been the worth of that primitive innocence portrayed in the myth of the garden of Eden, had it ever been realized in the life of men ?   What would have been the moral value or significance of a race of human beings ignorant of sin, and doing beneficent acts with no more consciousness or volition than the deftly contrived machine that picks up raw material at one end, and turns out some finished product at the other ?   Clearly, for strong and resolute men and women an Eden would be but a fool's paradise.   How could anything fit to be called *character* have ever been produced there ?   But for tasting the forbidden fruit, in what respect could man have become a being of higher order than the beasts of the field? An interesting question is this, for it leads us to consider the genesis of the idea of moral evil in man.

VII

A Word of Caution

EFORE we enter upon this topic a word of caution may be needed. I do not wish the purpose of the foregoing questions to be misunderstood. The serial nature of human thinking and speaking makes it impossible to express one's thought on any great subject in a solid block; one must needs give it forth in consecutive fragments, so that parts of it run the risk of being lost upon the reader or hearer, while other parts are made to assume undue proportions. Moreover, there are many minds that habitually catch at the fragments of a thought, and never seize it in the block; and in such manner do strange misconceptions arise. I never could have dreamed, until taught by droll experience, that the foregoing allusions to the garden of Eden could be understood as a glorification of sin, and an invitation to my fellow-men to come forth with me and be wicked! But even so it was, on one occasion when I was trying, somewhat more scantily than here, to state the present case. In the midst of my endeavour to justify the grand spirit of faith which our fathers showed when from abysmal depths of affliction they never failed to cry that God doeth all things well, I was suddenly interrupted with queries as to just what percentage of sin and crime I regarded as needful for the moral equilibrium of the universe; how much did I propose to commit myself, how much would I advise people in general to commit, and just where would I have them stop! Others deemed it necessary to remind me that there is already too much suffering in the world, and we ought not to seek to increase it; that the difference between right and wrong is of great practical importance; and that if we try to treat evil as good we shall make good no better than evil.

When one has sufficiently recovered one's gravity, it is permissible to reply to such criticisms that the sharp antithesis between good and evil is essential to every step of my argument, which would entirely collapse if the antagonism were for one moment disregarded. The quantity of suffering in the world is unquestionably so great as to prompt us to do all in our power to diminish it ; such we shall presently see must be the case in a world that proceeds through stages of evolution. When one reverently assumes that it was through some all-wise and holy purpose that sin was permitted to come into the world, it ought to be quite superfluous to add that the fulfilment of any such purpose demands that sin be not cherished, but suppressed. If one seeks, as a philosopher, to explain and justify God's wholesale use of death in the general economy of the universe, is one forsooth to be charged with praising murder as a fine art and with seeking to found a society of Thugs ?

VIII

The Hermit and the Angel

HE simple-hearted monks of the Middle Ages understood, in their own quaint way, that God's methods of governing this universe are not always fit to be imitated by his finite creatures. In one of the old stories that furnished entertainment and instruction for the cloister it is said that a hermit and an angel once journeyed together. The angel was in human form and garb, but had told his companion the secret of his exalted rank and nature. Coming at nightfall to a humble house by the wayside, the two travellers craved shelter for the love of God. A dainty supper and a soft, warm bed were given them, and in the middle of the night the angel arose and strangled the kind host's infant son, who was quietly sleeping

in his cradle. The good hermit was para-
lyzed with amazement and horror, but dared
not speak a word. The next night the two
comrades were entertained at a fine man-
sion in the city, where the angel stole the
superb golden cup from which his host had
quaffed wine at dinner. Next day, while
crossing the bridge over a deep and rapid
stream, a pilgrim met the travellers. "Canst
thou show us, good father," said the angel,
"the way to the next town?" As the
pilgrim turned to point it out, this terrible
being caught him by the shoulder and flung
him into the river to drown. "Verily,"
thought the poor hermit, "it is a devil that
I have here with me, and all his works are
evil;" but fear held his tongue, and the
twain fared on their way till the sun had
set and snow began to fall, and the howling
of wolves was heard in the forest hard by.
Presently the bright light coming from a
cheerful window gave hope of a welcome
refuge; but the surly master of the house
turned the travellers away from his door

with curses and foul gibes. "Yonder is
my pig-sty for dirty vagrants like you."
So they passed that night among the swine;
and in the morning the angel went to the
house and thanked the master for his hospi-
tality, and gave him for a keepsake (thrifty
angel!) the stolen goblet. Then did the
hermit's wrath and disgust overcome his
fears, and he loudly upbraided his companion. "Get thee gone, wretched spirit!"
he cried. "I will have no more of thee.
Thou pretendest to be a messenger from
heaven, yet thou requitest good with evil,
and evil with good!" Then did the angel
look upon him with infinite compassion in
his eyes. "Listen," said he, "short-sighted
mortal. The birth of that infant son had
made the father covetous, breaking God's
commandments in order to heap up trea-
sures which the boy, if he had lived, would
have wasted in idle debauchery. By my
act, which seemed so cruel, I saved both
parent and child. The owner of the goblet
had once been abstemious, but was fast

becoming a sot; the loss of his cup has set
him to thinking, and he will mend his ways.
The poor pilgrim, unknown to himself, was
about to commit a mortal sin, when I inter-
fered and sent his unsullied soul to heaven.
As for the wretch who drove God's children from his door, he is, indeed, pleased
for the moment with the bauble I left in
his hands; but hereafter he will burn in
hell." So spoke the angel; and when he
had heard these words the hermit bowed
his venerable head and murmured, "For-
give me, Lord, that in my ignorance I mis-
judged thee."

I suspect that, with all our boasted science, there is still much wisdom for us in
the humble childlike piety of the Gesta
Romanorum. To say that the ways of
Providence are inscrutable is still something more than an idle platitude, and
there still is room for the belief that, could
we raise the veil that enshrouds eternal
truth, we should see that behind nature's
cruelest works there are secret springs of

divinest tenderness and love. In this trust-
ful mood we may now return to the question as to the genesis of the idea of moral
evil, and its close connection with man's
rise from a state of primeval innocence.

IX

Man's Rise from the Innocence of Brutehood

E have first to note that in various ways the action of natural selection has been profoundly modified in the course of the development of mankind from a race of inferior creatures. One of the chief factors in the production of man was the change that occurred in the direction of the working of natural selection, whereby in the line of man's direct ancestry the variations in intelligence came to be seized upon, cherished, and enhanced, to the comparative neglect of variations in bodily structure. The physical differences between man and ape are less important than the physical differences between African and South American apes. The latter belong to different zoölogical families, but the former do not. Zoölogically, man is simply one genus in the old-world family of apes. Psychologically, he has travelled so far from apes that the distance is scarcely measurable. This transcendent contrast is primarily due to the change in the direction of the working of natural selection. The consequences of this change were numerous and far-reaching. One consequence was that gradual lengthening of the plastic period of infancy which enabled man to became a progressive creature, and organized the primeval semi-human horde into definite family groups. I have elsewhere expounded this point, and it is known as my own especial contribution to the theory of evolution.

Another associated consequence, which here more closely concerns us, was the partial stoppage of the process of natural selection in remedying unfitness. A quotation from Herbert Spencer will help us to understand this partial stoppage : " As fast as the faculties are multiplied, so fast does it become possible for the several mem-

bers of a species to have various kinds of
superiorities over one another.   While one
saves its life by higher speed, another does
the like by clearer vision, another by keener
scent, another by quicker hearing, another
by greater strength, another by unusual
power of enduring cold or hunger, another
by special sagacity, another by special timid-
ity, another by special courage. . . . Now
. . . each of these attributes, giving its possessor an extra chance of life, is likely to
be transmitted to posterity.   But " it is not
nearly so likely to be increased by natural
selection.   For "if those members of the
species which have but ordinary " or even
deficient shares of some valuable attribute
"nevertheless survive by virtue of other
superiorities which they severally possess,
then it is not easy to see how this particular attribute can be " enhanced in subsequent generations by natural selection.[1]

These considerations apply especially to
the human race with its multitudinous capa-

[1] Biology, i. 454.

cities, and I can better explain the case by a crude and imperfect illustration than by a detailed and elaborate statement. If an individual antelope falls below the average of the herd in speed, he is sure to become food for lions, and thus the high average of speed in the herd is maintained by natural selection. But if an individual man becomes a drunkard, though his capabilities be ever so much curtailed by this vice, yet the variety of human faculty furnishes so many hooks with which to keep one's hold upon life that he may sin long and flagrantly without perishing; and if the drunkard survives, the action of natural selection in weeding out drunkenness is checked. There is thus a wide interval between the highest and lowest degrees of completeness in living that are compatible with maintenance of life. Mankind has so many other qualities beside the bad ones, which enable it to subsist and achieve progress in spite of them, that natural selection — which always works through death — cannot come into play.

Now it is because of this *interval* between the highest and lowest degrees of completeness of living that are compatible with the mere maintenance of life, that men can be distinguished as morally bad or morally good.   In inferior animals, where there is no such interval, there is no developed morality or conscience, though in a few of the higher ones there are the germs of these things.   Morality comes upon the scene when there is an alternative offered of leading better lives or worse lives.   And just as up to this point the actions of the forefathers of mankind have been determined by the pursuit of pleasure and avoidance of pain, so now they begin to be practically determined by the pursuit of goodness and avoidance of evil.   This rise from a bestial to a moral plane of existence involves the acquirement of the knowledge of good and evil.   Conscience is generated to play a part analogous to that played by the sense of pain in the lower stages of life, and to keep us from wrong doing.   To the mere love of life, which is the conservative force that keeps the whole animal world in existence, there now comes gradually to be superadded the feeling of religious aspiration, which is nothing more nor less than the yearning after the highest possible completeness of spiritual life. In the lower stages of human development this religious aspiration has as yet but an embryonic existence, and moral obligations are still but imperfectly recognized. It is only after long ages of social discipline, fraught with cruel afflictions and grinding misery, that the moral law becomes dominant and religious aspiration intense and abiding in the soul. When such a stage is reached, we have at last in man a creature different in kind from his predecessors, and fit for an everlasting life of progress, for a closer and closer communion with God in beatitude that shall endure.

X

The Relativity of Evil

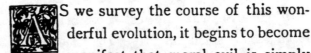S we survey the course of this wonderful evolution, it begins to become manifest that moral evil is simply the characteristic of the lower state of living as looked at from the higher state. Its existence is purely relative, yet it is profoundly real, and in a process of perpetual spiritual evolution its presence in some hideous form throughout a long series of upward stages is indispensable. Its absence would mean stagnation, quiescence, unprogressiveness. For the moment we exercise conscious choice between one course of action and another, we recognize the difference between better and worse, we foreshadow the whole grand contrast between good and bad. In the process of spiritual evolution, therefore, evil must needs be present. But

the nature of evolution also requires that it
should be evanescent. In the higher stages
that which is worse than the best need no
longer be positively bad. After the nature
of that which the upward-striving soul ab-
hors has been forever impressed upon it,
amid the long vicissitudes of its pilgrimage
through the dark realms of sin and expia-
tion, it is at length equipped for its final
sojourn

"In the blest kingdoms meek of joy and love."

From the general analogies furnished in the
process of evolution, we are entitled to hope
that, as it approaches its goal and man
comes nearer to God, the fact of evil will
lapse into a mere memory, in which the
shadowed past shall serve as a background
for the realized glory of the present.

Thus we have arrived at the goal of my
argument. We can at least begin to realize
distinctly that unless our eyes had been
opened at some time, so that we might
come to know the good and the evil, we
should never have become fashioned in

God's image. We should have been the denizens of a world of puppets, where neither morality nor religion could have found place or meaning. The mystery of evil remains a mystery still, but it is no longer a harsh dissonance such as greeted the poet's ear when the doors of hell were thrown open; for we see that this mystery belongs among the profound harmonies in God's creation. This reflection may have in it something that is consoling as we look forth upon the ills of the world. Many are the pains of life, and the struggle with wickedness is hard; its course is marked with sorrow and tears. But assuredly its deep impress upon the human soul is the indispensable background against which shall be set hereafter the eternal joys of heaven!

THE COSMIC ROOTS OF LOVE
AND SELF–SACRIFICE

———•———

O abbondante grazia, ond' io presunsi
   Ficcar lo viso per la luce eterna
   Tanto, che la veduta vi consunsi!
Nel suo profondo vidi che s' interna,
   Legato con amore in un volume,
   Ciò che per l' universo si squaderna.
               DANTE, *Paradiso*, xxxiii. 82.

I

The Summer Field, and what it tells us

HERE are few sights in Nature more restful to the soul than a daisied field in June. Whether it be at the dewy hour of sunrise, with blithe matin songs still echoing among the tree-tops, or while the luxuriant splendour of noontide fills the delicate tints of the early foliage with a pure glory of light, or in that more pensive time when long shadows are thrown eastward and the fresh breath of the sea is felt, or even under the solemn mantle of darkness, when all forms have faded from sight and the night air is musical with the murmurs of innumerable insects, amid all the varying moods through which the daily cycle runs, the abiding sense is of unalloyed happiness, the profound tranquillity of mind and heart that nothing ever brings save the contemplation of perfect beauty.   One's thought is carried back for the moment to that morning of the world when God looked upon his work and saw that it was good.   If in the infinite and eternal Creative Energy one might imagine some inherent impulse perpetually urging toward fresh creation, what could it be more likely to be than the divine contentment in giving objective existence to the boundless and subtle harmonies whereof our world is made ?   That it is a world of perfect harmony and unsullied beauty, who can doubt as he strolls through this summer field ?   As our thought plays lightly with its sights and sounds, there is nothing but gladness in the laugh of the bobolink ; the thrush's tender note tells only of the sweet domestic companionship of the nest ; creeping and winged things emerging from their grubs fill us with the sense of abounding life ; and the myriad buttercups, hallowed with vague memories of June days in

childhood, lose none of their charm in re-
minding us of the profound sympathy and
mutual dependence in which the worlds of
flowers and insects have grown up. The
blades of waving grass, the fluttering leaves
upon the lilac bush, appeal to us with rare
fascination ; for the green stuff that fills
their cellular tissues, and the tissues of all
green things that grow, is the world's great
inimitable worker of wonders ; its marvellous alchemy takes dead matter and breathes
into it the breath of life. But for that magician chlorophyll, conjuring with sunbeams,
such things as animal life and conscious intelligence would be impossible ; there would
be no problems of creation, nor philosopher
to speculate upon them. Thus the delight
that sense impression gives, as we wander
among buttercups and daisies, becomes
deepened into gratitude and veneration, till
we quite understand how the rejuvenescence
of Nature should in all ages have aroused
men to acts of worship, and should call forth
from modern masters of music, the most

religious of the arts of expression, outbursts
of sublimest song.

And yet we need but come a little closer
to the facts to find them apparently telling
us a very different story. The moment we
penetrate below the superficial aspect of
things the scene is changed. In the folk-
lore of Ireland there is a widespread belief
in a fairyland of eternal hope and bright-
ness and youth situated a little way below the
roots of the grass. From that land of Tir
nan Og, as the peasants call it, the secret
springs of life shoot forth their scions in
this visible world, and thither a few favoured
mortals have now and then found their way.
It is into no blest country of Tir nan Og
that our stern science leads us, but into a
scene of ugliness and hatred, strife and
massacre. Macaulay tells of the battlefield
of Neerwinden, that the next summer after
that frightful slaughter the whole country-
side was densely covered with scarlet pop-
pies, which people beheld with awe as a
token of wrath in heaven over the deeds

wrought on earth by human passions. Any
summer field, though mantled in softest
green, is the scene of butchery as wholesale
as that of Neerwinden and far more ruth-
less. The life of its countless tiny denizens
is one of unceasing toil, of crowding and
jostling, where the weaker fall unpitied by
the way, of starvation from hunger and
cold, of robbery utterly shameless and murder utterly cruel. That green sward in
taking possession of its territory has exter-
minated scores of flowering plants of the
sort that human economics and æsthetics
stigmatize as weeds; nor do the blades of
the victorious army dwell side by side in
amity, but in their eagerness to dally with
the sunbeams thrust aside and supplant
one another without the smallest compunc-
tion. Of the crawling insects and those
that hum through the air, with the quaint
snail, the burrowing worm, the bloated toad,
scarce one in a hundred but succumbs to
the buffets of adverse fortune before it has
achieved maturity and left offspring to re-

place it.   The early bird, who went forth in quest of the worm, was lucky if at the close of a day as full of strife and peril as ever knight-errant encountered, he did not himself serve as a meal for some giant foe in the gloaming.   When we think of the hawk's talons buried in the breast of the wren, while the relentless beak tears the little wings from the quivering, bleeding body, our mood toward Nature is changed, and we feel like recoiling from a world in which such black injustice, such savage disregard for others, is part of the general scheme.

II

Seeming Wastefulness of the Cosmic Process

BUT as we look still further into the matter, our mood is changed once more. We find that this hideous hatred and strife, this wholesale famine and death, furnish the indispensable conditions for the evolution of higher and higher types of life. Nay more, but for the pitiless destruction of all individuals that fall short of a certain degree of fitness to the circumstances of life into which they are born, the type would inevitably degenerate, the life would become lower and meaner in kind. Increase in richness, variety, complexity of life is gained only by the selection of variations above or beyond a certain mean, and the prompt execution of a death sentence upon all the rest. The principle of natural selection is in one respect intensely Calvinistic; it elects the one and damns the ninety and nine. In these processes of Nature there is nothing that savours of communistic equality; but "to him that hath shall be given, and from him that hath not shall be taken away even that which he hath." Through this selection of a favoured few, a higher type of life — or at all events a type in which there is more life — is attained in many cases, but not always. Evolution and progress are not synonymous terms. The survival of the fittest is not always a survival of the best or of the most highly organized. The environment is sometimes such that increase of fitness means degeneration of type, and the animal and vegetable worlds show many instances of degeneration. One brilliant instance is that which has preserved the clue to the remote ancestry of the vertebrate type. The molluscoid ascidian, rooted polyp-like on the sea beach in shallow water, has an embryonic history which shows that its ancestors had once seen better days, when they darted to and

fro, fishlike, through the waves, with the prophecy of a vertebrate skeleton within them.
This is a case of marked degeneration.
More often survival of the fittest simply
preserves the type unchanged through long
periods of time. But now and then under
favourable circumstances it raises the type.
At all events, whenever the type is raised,
it is through survival of the fittest, implying
destruction of all save the fittest.

This last statement is probably true of
all plants and of all animals except that
as applied to the human race it needs some
transcendently important qualifications
which students of evolution are very apt to
neglect. I shall by and by point out these
qualifications. At present we may note
that the development of civilization, on its
political side, has been a stupendous struggle for life, wherein the possession of certain physical and mental attributes has
enabled some tribes or nations to prevail
over others, and to subject or exterminate
them. On its industrial side the struggle

has been no less fierce ; the evolution of higher efficiency through merciless competition is a matter of common knowledge. Alike in the occupations of war and in those of peace, superior capacity has thriven upon victories in which small heed has been paid to the wishes or the welfare of the vanquished.   In human history perhaps no relation has been more persistently repeated than that of the hawk and the wren.   The aggression has usually been defended as in the interests of higher civilization, and in the majority of cases the defence has been sustained by the facts.   It has indeed very commonly been true that the survival of the strongest is the survival of the fittest.

Such considerations affect our mood toward Nature in a way that is somewhat bewildering. On the one hand, as we recognize in the universal strife and slaughter a stern discipline through which the standard of animate existence is raised and the life of creatures variously enriched, we become to some extent reconciled to the facts. Assuming, as we all do, that the attainment of higher life is in itself desirable, our minds cannot remain utterly inhospitable towards things, however odious in themselves, that help toward the desirable end. Since we cannot rid the world of them, we acquiesce in their existence as part of the machinery of God's providence, the intricacies of which our finite minds cannot hope to unravel. On the other hand, a thought is likely to arise which in days gone by we should have striven to suppress as too impious for utterance ; but it is wiser to let such thoughts find full expression, for only thus can we be sure of understanding the kind of problem we are trying to solve. Is not, then, this method of Nature, which achieves progress only through misery and death, an exceedingly brutal and clumsy method ? Life, one would think, must be dear to the everlasting Giver of life, yet how cheap it seems to be held in the general scheme of things ! In order that some race of moths may at-

tain a certain fantastic contour and marking
of their wings, untold thousands of moths
are doomed to perish prematurely. Instead
of making the desirable object once for all,
the method of Nature is to make something
else and reject it, and so on through countless ages, till by slow approximations the
creative thought is realized. Nature is
often called thrifty, yet could anything be
more prodigal or more cynical than the
waste of individual lives? Does it not remind one of Charles Lamb's famous story
of the Chinaman whose house accidentally
burned down and roasted a pig, whereupon
the dainty meat was tasted and its fame
spread abroad until epicures all over China
were to be seen carrying home pigs and
forthwith setting fire to their houses? We
need but add that the custom thus established lasted for centuries, during which
every dinner of pig involved the sacrifice of
a homestead, and we seem to have a close
parody upon the wastefulness of Nature, or
of what is otherwise called in these days

the Cosmic Process. Upon such a view
as this the Cosmic Process appears in a
high degree unintelligent, not to say immoral.

III

Caliban's Philosophy

OLYTHEISM easily found a place for such views as these, inasmuch as it could explain the unseemly aspects of Nature offhand by a reference to malevolent deities. With Browning's Caliban, in his meditations upon Setebos, that god whom he conceived in his own image, the recklessness of Nature is mockery engendered half in spite, half in mere wantonness. Setebos, he says,

> " is strong and Lord,
> Am strong myself compared to yonder crabs
> That march now from the mountain to the sea ;
> Let twenty pass, and stone the twenty-first,
> Loving not, hating not, just choosing so.
> Say, the first straggler that boasts purple spots
> Shall join the file, one pincer twisted off ;
> Say, this bruised fellow shall receive a worm,
> And two worms he whose nippers end in red ;
> As it likes me each time, I do : So He."

Such is the kind of philosophy that commends itself to the beastly Caliban, as he sprawls in the mire with small eft things creeping down his back. His half-fledged mind can conceive no higher principle of action — nothing more artistic, nothing more masterful — than wanton mockery, and naturally he attributes it to his God; it is for him a sufficient explanation of that little fragment of the Cosmic Process with which he comes into contact.

IV

Can it be that the Cosmic Process has no Relation to Moral Ends?

UT as long as we confine our attention to the universal struggle for life and the survival of the fittest, without certain qualifications presently to be mentioned, it is difficult for the most profound intelligence to arrive at conclusions much more satisfactory than Caliban's. If the spirit shown in Nature's works as thus contemplated is not one of wanton mockery, it seems at any rate to be a spirit of stolid indifference. It indicates a Blind Force rather than a Beneficent Wisdom at the source of things. It is in some such mood as this that Huxley tells us, in his famous address delivered at Oxford, in 1893, that there is no sanction for morality in the Cosmic Process. "Men in

society," he says, " are undoubtedly subject
to the cosmic process. As among other
animals, multiplication goes on without ces-
sation and involves severe competition for
the means of support. The struggle for
existence tends to eliminate those less
fitted to adapt themselves to the circumstances of their existence. The strongest,
the most self-assertive, tend to tread down
the weaker. . . . Social progress means a
checking of the cosmic process at every
step and the substitution for it of another,
which may be called the ethical process;
the end of which is not the survival of
those who may happen to be the fittest,
in respect of the whole of the conditions
which exist, but of those who are ethically
the best." Again, says Huxley, " let us
understand, once for all, that the ethical
progress of society depends, not on imi-
tating the cosmic process, still less in run-
ning away from it, but in combating it."
And again he tells us that while the moral
sentiments have undoubtedly been evolved,

yet since "the immoral sentiments have no less been evolved, there is so far as much natural sanction for the one as for the other." And yet again, "the cosmic process has no sort of relation to moral ends."

When these statements were first made they were received with surprise, and they have since called forth much comment, for they sound like a retreat from the position which an evolutionist is expected to hold. They distinctly assert a breach of continuity between evolution in general and the evolution of Man in particular; and thus they have carried joy to the hearts of sundry theologians, of the sort that like to regard Man as an infringer upon Nature. If there is no natural sanction for morality, then the sanction must be supernatural, and forthwith such theologians greet Huxley as an ally!

They are mistaken, however. Huxley does not really mean to assert any such breach of continuity as is here suggested. In a footnote to his printed address he makes a qualification which really cancels the group of statements I have quoted. "Of course," says Huxley, "strictly speaking, social life and the ethical process, in virtue of which it advances toward perfection, are part and parcel of the general process of evolution." Of course they are; and of course the general process of evolution is the cosmic process, it is Nature's way of doing things. But when my dear Huxley a moment ago was saying that the "cosmic process has no sort of relation to moral ends," he was using the phrase in a more restricted sense; he was using it as equivalent to what Darwin called "natural selection," what Spencer called "survival of the fittest," which is only one part of the cosmic process. Now most assuredly survival of the fittest, as such, has no sort of relation to moral ends. Beauty and ugliness, virtue and vice, are all alike to it. Side by side with the exquisite rose flourishes the hideous tarantula, and in too many cases the villain's chances of livelihood are

better than the saint's.   As I said a while
ago, if we confine our attention to the
survival of the fittest in the struggle for
existence, we are not likely to arrive at
conclusions much more satisfactory than
Caliban's

"As it likes me each time, I do : So He."

In such a universe we may look in vain
for any sanction for morality, any justification for love and self-sacrifice ; we find no
hope in it, no consolation ; there is not
even dignity in it, nothing whatever but
resistless all-producing and all-consuming
energy.

Such a universe, however, is not the one
in which we live.   In the cosmic process of
evolution, whereof our individual lives are
part and parcel, there are other agencies
at work besides natural selection, and the
story of the struggle for existence is far
from being the whole story.   I have thus
far been merely stating difficulties ; it is
now time to point out the direction in
which we are to look for a solution of

them. I think it can be shown that the
principles of morality have their roots in
the deepest foundations of the universe,
that the cosmic process is ethical in the
profoundest sense, that in that far-off morning of the world, when the stars sang together and the sons of God shouted for
joy, the beauty of self-sacrifice and disinterested love formed the chief burden of
the mighty theme.

V

First Stages in the Genesis of Man

ET us begin by drawing a correct though slight outline sketch of what the cosmic process of evolution has been. It is not strange that when biologists speak of evolution they should often or usually have in mind simply the modifications wrought in plants and animals by means of natural selection. For it was by calling attention to such modifications that Darwin discovered a true cause of the origin of species by physiological descent from allied species. Thus was demonstrated the fact of evolution in its most important province; men of science were convinced that the higher forms of life are derived from lower forms, and the old notion of special creations was exploded once and forever. This was a great scientific achievement, one of the greatest known to history, and it is therefore not strange that language should often be employed as if Evolutionism and Darwinism were synonymous. Yet not only are there extensive regions in the doctrine of evolution about which Darwin knew very little, but even as regards the genesis of species his theory was never developed in his own hands so far as to account satisfactorily for the genesis of man.

It must be borne in mind that while the natural selection of physical variations will go far toward explaining the characteristics of all the plants and all the beasts in the world, it remains powerless to account for the existence of man. Natural selection of physical variations might go on for a dozen eternities without any other visible result than new forms of plant and beast in endless and meaningless succession. The physical variations by which man is distinguished from apes are not great. His physical relationship with the ape is closer than that between cat and dog, which belong to different families of the same order; it is more like that between cat and leopard, or between dog and fox, different genera in the same family. But the moment we consider the minds of man and ape, the gap between the two is immeasurable. Mr. Mivart has truly said that, with regard to their total value in nature, the difference between man and ape transcends the difference between ape and blade of grass. I should be disposed to go further and say, that while for zoölogical man you can hardly erect a distinct family from that of the chimpanzee and orang, on the other hand, for psychological man you must erect a distinct kingdom; nay, you must even dichotomize the universe, putting Man on one side and all things else on the other. How can this overwhelming contrast between psychical and physical difference be accounted for? The clue was furnished by Alfred Russel Wallace, the illustrious co-discoverer of natural selection. Wallace

saw that along with the general development of mammalian intelligence a point
must have been reached in the history of
one of the primates, when variations of intelligence were more profitable to him than
variations in body. From that time forth
that primate's intelligence went on by slow
increments acquiring new capacity, while
his body changed but little. When once
he could strike fire, and chip a flint, and
use a club, and strip off the bear's hide to
cover himself, there was clearly no further
use in thickening his own hide, or lengthening and sharpening his claws. Natural
selection is the keenest capitalist in the
universe ; she never loses an instant in
seizing the most profitable place for invest-
ment, and her judgment is never at fault.
Forthwith, for a million years or more she
invested all her capital in the psychical
variations of this favoured primate, making
little change in his body except so far as to
aid in the general result, until by and by
something like human intelligence of a low

grade, like that of the Australian or the Andaman islander, was achieved. The genesis of humanity was by no means yet completed, but an enormous gulf had been crossed.

After throwing out this luminous suggestion Mr. Wallace never followed it up as it admitted and deserved. It is too much to expect one man to do everything, and his splendid studies in the geographical distribution of organisms may well have left him little time for work in this direction. Who can fail to see that the selection of psychical variations, to the comparative neglect of physical variations, was the opening of a new and greater act in the drama of creation? Since that new departure the Creator's highest work has consisted not in bringing forth new types of body, but in expanding and perfecting the psychical attributes of the one creature in whose life those attributes have begun to acquire predominance. Along this human line of ascent there is no occasion for any further

genesis of species, all future progress must
continue to be not zoölogical, but psychological, organic evolution gives place to
civilization.   Thus in the long series of
organic beings Man is the last ; the cosmic
process, having once evolved this master-
piece, could thenceforth do nothing better
than to perfect him.

VI

The Central Fact in the Genesis of Man

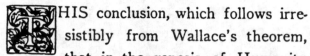HIS conclusion, which follows irre-
sistibly from Wallace's theorem,
that in the genesis of Humanity
natural selection began to follow a new
path, already throws a light of promise over
our whole subject, like the rosy dawn of a
June morning. But the explanation of the
genesis of Humanity is still far from complete. If we compare man with any of the
higher mammals, such as dogs and horses
and apes, we are struck with several points
of difference : *first*, the greater progressive-
ness of man, the widening of the interval
by which one generation may vary from its
predecessor ; *secondly*, the definite grouping
in societies based on more or less permanent family relationships, instead of the in-
definite grouping in miscellaneous herds or

packs ; *thirdly*, the possession of articulate
speech ; *fourthly*, the enormous increase in
the duration of infancy, or the period when
parental care is needed. Twenty-four years
ago, in a course of lectures given yonder in
Holden Chapel, I showed that the circumstance last named is the fundamental one,
and the others are derivative. It is the
prolonged infancy that has caused the pro-
gressiveness and the grouping into definite
societies, while the development of language
was a consequence of the increasing intelligence and sociality thus caused. In the
genesis of Humanity the central fact has
been the increased duration of infancy.
Now, can we assign for that increased duration an adequate cause? I think we can.
The increase of intelligence is itself such a
cause. A glance at the animal kingdom
shows us no such thing as infancy among
the lower orders. · It is with warm-blooded
birds and mammals that the phenomena
of infancy and the correlative parental care
really begin.

VII

The Chief Cause of Man's lengthened Infancy

HE reason for this is that any creature's ability to perceive and to act depends upon the registration of experiences in his nerve-centres. It is either individual or ancestral experience that is thus registered; or, strictly speaking, it is both. It is of the first importance that this point should be clearly understood, and therefore a few words of elementary explanation will not be superfluous.

When you learn to play the piano, you gradually establish innumerable associations between printed groups of notes and the corresponding keys on the key-board, and you also train the fingers to execute a vast number of rapid and complicated motions. The process is full of difficulty, and involves

endless repetition. After some years perhaps you can play at sight and with almost
automatic ease a polonaise of Liszt or a
ballad of Chopin. Now this result is possible only because of a bodily change which
has taken place in you. Countless molecular alterations have been wrought in the
structure of sundry nerves and muscles,
especially in the gray matter of sundry gan-
glia, or nerve-centres. Every ganglion concerned in the needful adjustments of eyes
and fingers and wrists, or in the perception
of musical sounds, has undergone a change
more or less profound. The nature of the
change is largely a matter of speculation;
but that point need not in any way concern
us. It is enough for us to know that there
is such a change, and that it is a registration of experiences. The pianist has registered in the intimate structure of his nervous system a world of experiences entirely
foreign to persons unfamiliar with the piano;
and upon this registration his capacity depends.

Now the same explanation applies to all bodily movements whatever, whether complicated or simple. In writing, in walking, in talking, we are making use of nervous registrations that have been brought about by an accumulation of experiences. To pick up a pencil from the table may seem a very simple act, yet a baby cannot do it. It has been made possible only by the education of the eyes, of the muscles that move the eyes, of the arm and hand, and of the nerve-centres that coördinate one group of movements with another. All this multiform education has consisted in a gradual registration of experiences. In like manner all the actions of man upon the world about him are made up of movements, and every such movement becomes possible only when a registration is effected in sundry nerve-centres.

But this is not the whole story. The case is undoubtedly the same with those visceral movements, involuntary and in great part unconscious, which sustain life;

the beating of the heart, the expansion and contraction of the lungs, the slight changes of calibre in the blood-vessels, even the movements of secretion that take place in glands. All these actions are governed by nerves, and these nerves have had to be educated to their work. This education has been a registration of experiences chiefly ancestral, throughout an enormous past, practically since the beginnings of vertebrate life.

With the earlier and simpler forms of animal existence these visceral movements are the only ones, or almost the only ones, that have to be made. Presently the movements of limbs and sense organs come to be added, and as we rise in the animal scale, these movements come to be endlessly various and complex, and by and by implicate the nervous system more and more deeply in complex acts of perception, memory, reasoning, and volition. Obviously, therefore, in the development of the individual organism the demands of the nervous system upon the vital energies concerned in growth must come to be of paramount importance, and in providing for them the entire embryonic life must be most profoundly and variously affected. Though we may be unable to follow the processes in detail, the truth of this general statement is plain and undeniable.

I say, then, that when a creature's intelligence is low, and its experience very meagre, consisting of a few simple perceptions and acts that occur throughout life with monotonous regularity, all the registration of this experience gets effected in the nerve-centres of its offspring before birth, and they come into the world fully equipped for the battle of life, like the snapping turtle, which snaps with decisive vigour as soon as it emerges from the egg. Nothing is left plastic to be finished after birth, and so the life of each generation is almost an exact repetition of its predecessor. But when a creature's intelligence is high, and its experience varied and complicated, the registration of all this experience in the nerve-centres of its off-spring does not get accomplished before birth. There is not time enough. The most important registrations, such as those needed for breathing and swallowing and other indispensable acts, are fully effected; others, such as those needed for handling and walking, are but partially effected; others, such as those involved in the recognition of creatures not important as enemies or prey, are left still further from completion. Much is left to be done by individual experience after birth. The animal, when first born, is a baby dependent upon its mother's care. At the same time its intelligence is far more plastic, and it remains far more teachable, than the lower animal that has no babyhood. Dogs and horses, lions and elephants, often increase in sagacity until late in life; and so do apes, which, along with a higher intelligence than any other dumb animals, have a much longer babyhood.

We are now prepared to appreciate the

marvellous beauty of Nature's work in bringing Man upon the scene.   Nowhere is there
any breach of continuity in the cosmic process.   First we have natural selection at
work throughout the organic world, bringing forth millions of species of plant and
animal, seizing upon every advantage, physical or mental, that enables any species
to survive in the universal struggle.   So
far as any outward observer, back in the
Cretaceous or early Eocene periods, could
surmise, this sort of confusion might go on
forever.   But all at once, perhaps somewhere in the upper Eocene or lower Mio-
cene, it appears that among the primates,
a newly developing family already distinguished for prehensile capabilities, one
genus is beginning to sustain itself more
by mental craft and shiftiness than by any
physical characteristic.   Forthwith does
natural selection seize upon any and every
advantageous variation in this craft and
shiftiness, until this favoured genus of primates, this *Homo Alalus*, or speechless

man, as we may call him, becomes pre-
eminent for sagacity, as the mammoth is
preëminent for bulk, or the giraffe for
length of neck.

VIII

Some of its Effects

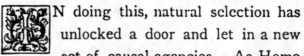N doing this, natural selection has unlocked a door and let in a new set of causal agencies. As Homo Alalus grows in intelligence and variety of experience, his helpless babyhood becomes gradually prolonged, and passes not into sudden maturity, but into a more or less plastic intermediate period of youth. Individual experience, as contrasted with ancestral experience, counts for much more than ever before in shaping his actions, and thus he begins to become progressive. He can learn many more new ways of doing things in a hundred thousand years than any other creature could have done in a much longer time. Thus the rate of progress is enhanced, the increasing intelligence of Homo Alalus further lengthens

his plastic period of life, and this in turn
further increases his intelligence and em-
phasizes his individuality. The evidence is
abundant that Homo Alalus, like his simian
cousins, was a gregarious creature, and it
is not difficult to see how, with increasing
intelligence, the gestures and grunts used
in the horde for signalling must come to be
clothed with added associations of meaning,
must gradually become generalized as signs
of conceptions. This invention of spoken
language, the first invention of nascent
humanity, remains to this day its most
fruitful invention. Henceforth ancestral
experience could not simply be transmitted
through its inheritable impress upon the
nervous system, but its facts and lessons
could become external materials and instruments of education. Then the children of
Homo Alalus, no longer speechless, began
to accumulate a fund of tradition, which in
the fulness of time was to bloom forth in
history and poetry, in science and theology.
From the outset the acquisition of speech

must greatly have increased the rate of progress, and enhanced the rudimentary sociality.

With the lengthening of infancy the period of maternal help and watchfulness must have lengthened in correspondence. Natural selection must keep those two things nicely balanced, or the species would soon become extinct. But Homo Alalus had not only a mother, but brethren and sisters; and when the period of infancy became sufficiently long, there were a series of Homunculi Alali, the eldest of whom still needed more or less care while the third and the fourth were arriving upon the scene. In this way the sentiment of maternity became abiding. The cow has strong feelings of maternal affection for periods of a few weeks at a time, but lapses into indifference and probably cannot distinguish her grown-up calves as sustaining any nearer relation to herself than other members of the herd. But Femina Alala, with her vastly enlarged intelligence, is called upon for the exercise of maternal affection until it becomes a permanent part of her nature.   In the same group of circumstances begins the permanency of the marital relation.   The warrior - hunter grows accustomed to defending the same wife and children and to helping them in securing food.   Cases of what we may term wedlock, arising in this way, occur sporadically among apes ; its thorough establishment, however, was not achieved until after the genesis of Humanity had been completed in most other respects.   The elaborate researches of Westermarck have proved that permanent marriage exists even among savages ; it did not prevail, however, until the advanced stage of culture represented by the Aztecs in aboriginal America and the Neolithic peoples of ancient Europe. As for strict monogamy, it is a comparatively late achievement of civilization. What the increased and multiplied duration of infancy at first accomplished was the transformation of miscellaneous hordes

of Homines Alali into organized clans re-
cognizing kinship through the mother, as
exemplified among nearly all American
Indians when observed by Europeans.

Thus by gradual stages we have passed
from four-footed existence into Human Society, and once more I would emphasize
the fact that nowhere do we find any breach
of continuity, but one factor sets another
in operation, which in turn reacts upon the
first, and so on in a marvellously harmo-
nious consensus. Surely if there is anywhere in the universe a story matchless for
its romantic interest, it is the story of the
genesis of Man, now that we are at length
beginning to be able to decipher it. We
see that there is a good deal more in it
than mere natural selection. At bottom,
indeed, it is all a process of survival of the
fittest, but the secondary agencies we have
been considering have brought us to a point
where our conception of the Struggle for
Life must be enlarged. Out of the mani-
fold compounding and recompounding of

primordial clans have come the nations of mankind in various degrees of civilization, but already in the clan we find the ethical process at work. The clan has a code of morals well adapted to the conditions amid which it exists. There is an ethical sentiment in the clan; its members have duties toward it; it punishes sundry acts even with death, and rewards or extols sundry other acts. We are, in short, in an ethical atmosphere, crude and stifling, doubtless, as compared with that of a modern Christian homestead, but still unquestionably ethical.

IX

Origin of Moral Ideas and Sentiments

OW, here at last, in encountering the ethical process at work, have we detected a breach of continuity? Has the moral sentiment been flung in from outside, or is it a natural result of the cosmic process we have been sketching? Clearly it is the latter. There has been no breach of continuity. When the prolongation of infancy produced the clan, there naturally arose reciprocal necessities of behaviour among the members of the clan, its mothers and children, its hunters and warriors. If such reciprocal necessities were to be disregarded the clan would dissolve, and dissolution would be general destruction. For, bear in mind, the clan, when once evolved, becomes the unit whose preservation is henceforth the permanent

necessity. It is infancy that has made it
so. A miscellaneous horde, with brief in-
fancies for its younger members, may survive a very extensive slaughter; but in a
clan, where the proportion of helpless children is much greater, and a considerable
division of labour between nurses and warriors has become established, the case is
different. An amount or degree of calam-
ity sufficient to break up its organization
will usually mean total ruin. Hence, when
Nature's travail has at length brought forth
the clan, its requirements forthwith become
paramount, and each member's conduct
from babyhood must conform to them.
Natural selection henceforth invests her
chief capital in the enterprise of preserving
the clan. In that primitive social unit lie
all the potentiality and promise of Human
Society through untold future ages. So
for age after age those clans in which the
conduct of the individuals is best subordi-
nated to the general welfare are sure to
prevail over clans in which the subordina-

tion is less perfect. As the maternal instinct had been cultivated for thousands
of generations before clanship came into
existence, so for many succeeding ages of
turbulence the patriotic instinct, which
prompts to the defence of home, was cultivated under penalty of death. Clans defended by weakly loyal or cowardly warriors were sure to perish. Unflinching
bravery and devoted patriotism were virtues
necessary to the survival of the community,
and were thus preserved until at the dawn
of historic times, in the most grandly mili-
tant of clan societies, we find the word
virtus connoting just these qualities, and
no sooner does the fateful gulf yawn open
in the forum than a Curtius joyfully leaps
into it, that the commonwealth may be
preserved from harm.

Now the moment a man's voluntary actions are determined by conscious or unconscious reference to a standard outside
of himself and his selfish motives, he has
entered the world of ethics, he has begun

to live in a moral atmosphere. Egoism has ceased to be all in all, and altruism — it is an ugly-sounding word, but seems to be the only one available — altruism has begun to assert its claim to sovereignty. In the earlier and purely animal stages of existence it was right enough for each individual to pursue pleasure and avoid pain ; it did not endanger the welfare of the species, but on the contrary it favoured that welfare ; in its origin avoidance of pain was the surest safeguard for the perpetuation of life, and with due qualifications that is still the case. But as soon as sociality became established, and Nature's supreme end became the maintenance of the clan organization, the standard for the individual's conduct became shifted, permanently and forever shifted. Limits were interposed at which pleasure must be resigned and pain endured, even certain death encountered, for the sake of the clan ; perhaps the individual did not always understand it in that way, but at all events it was for the sake of some rule recognized in the clan, some rule which, as his mother and all his kin had from his earliest childhood inculcated upon him, *ought* to be obeyed. This conception of ought, of obligation, of duty, of debt to something outside of self, resulted from the shifting of the standard of conduct outside of the individual's self. Once thus externalized, objectivized, the ethical standard demanded homage from the individual. It furnished the rule for a higher life than one dictated by mere selfishness. Speaking after the manner of naturalists, I here use the phrase " higher life " advisedly. It was the kind of life that was conducive to the preservation and further development of the highest form of animate existence that had been attained. It appears to me that we begin to find for ethics the most tremendous kind of sanction in the nature of the cosmic process.

A word of caution may be needed. It is not for a moment to be supposed that when primitive men began crudely shaping their

conduct with reference to a standard outside of self, they did so as the result of
meditation, or with any realizing sense of
what they were doing. That has never
been the method of evolution. Its results
steal upon the world noiselessly and unob-
served, and only after they have long been
with us does reason employ itself upon
them. The wolf does not eat the lamb because he regards a flesh diet as necessary
to his health and activity, but because he is
hungry, and, like Mr. Harold Skimpole, he
likes lamb. It was no intellectual perception of needs and consequences that lengthened the maternal instinct with primeval
mothers as the period of infancy lengthened. Nor was it any such intellectual
perception that began to enthrone "I
ought" in the place of "I wish." If in
the world's recurrent crises Nature had
waited to be served by the flickering lamp
of reason, the story would not have been
what it is. Her method has been, with the
advent of a new situation, to modify the

existing group of instincts; and this work
she will not let be slighted; in her train
follows the lictor with the symbols of death,
and there is neither pity nor relenting.   In
the primeval warfare between clans, those
in which the instincts were not so modified
as to shift the standard of conduct outside
of the individual's self must inevitably have
succumbed and perished under the pressure
of those in which the instincts had begun
to experience such modification.   The
moral law grew up in the world not because
anybody asked for it, but because it was
needed for the world's work.   If it is not a
product of the cosmic process, it would be
hard to find anything that could be so
called.

X

*The Cosmic Process exists purely for the Sake
of Moral Ends*

 HAVE not undertaken to make my outline sketch of the genesis of Humanity approach to completeness, but only to present enough salient points to make a closely connected argument in showing how morality is evolved in the cosmic process and sanctioned by it. In a more complete sketch it would be necessary to say something about the genesis of Religion. One of the most interesting, and in my opinion one of the most profoundly significant, facts in the whole process of evolution is the first appearance of religious sentiment at very nearly the same stage at which the moral law began to grow up. To the differential attributes of Humanity already considered there needs

to be added the possession of religious sentiment and religious ideas.   We may safely
say that this is the most important of all
the distinctions between Man and other
animals ; for to say so is simply to epito-
mize the whole of human experience as re-
corded in history, art, and literature.   Along
with the rise from gregariousness to incipient sociality, along with the first stammer-
ings of articulate speech, along with the
dawning discrimination between right and
wrong, came the earliest feeble groping
toward a world beyond that which greets
the senses, the first dim recognition of the
Spiritual Power that is revealed in and
through the visible and palpable realm of
nature.   And universally since that time
the notion of Ethics has been inseparably
associated with the notion of Religion, and
the sanction for Ethics has been held to be
closely related with the world beyond phenomena.   There   are   philosophers   who
maintain that with the further progress of
enlightenment this close relation will cease

to be asserted, that Ethics will be divorced from Religion, and that the groping of the Human Soul after its God will be condemned as a mere survival from the errors of primitive savagery, a vain and idle reaching out toward a world of mere phantoms. I mention this opinion merely to express unqualified and total dissent from it. I believe it can be shown that one of the strongest implications of the doctrine of evolution is the Everlasting Reality of Religion.

But we have not time at present for entering upon so vast a subject. Let this reference suffice to show that it has not been passed over or forgotten in my theory of the genesis of Humanity. In an account of the evolution of the religious sentiment, its first appearance as coeval, or nearly so, with the beginnings of the ethical process would assume great importance. We have here been concerned purely with the ethical process itself, which we have found to be — as Huxley truly says in his footnote — part and parcel of the general process

of evolution.   Our historical survey of the
genesis of Humanity seems to show very
forcibly that a society of Human Souls
living in conformity to a perfect Moral Law
is the end toward which, ever since the
time when our solar system was a patch of
nebulous vapour, the cosmic process has
been aiming.   After our cooling planet had
become the seat of organic life, the process
of natural selection went on for long ages
seemingly, but not really at random; for
our retrospect shows that its ultimate tendency was towards singling out one creature and exalting his intelligence.

Now we have seen that this increase of intelligence itself, by entailing upon Man the
helplessness of infancy, led directly to the
production of those social conditions that
called the ethical process into play and set
it actively to work.   Thus we may see the
absurdity of trying to separate the moral
nature of Man from the rest of his nature,
and to assign for it a separate and independent history.   The essential solidarity

in the cosmic process will admit of no
such fanciful detachment of one part from
another.   All parts are involved one in
another.   Again, the ethical process is not
only part and parcel of the cosmic process,
but it is its crown and consummation.
Toward the spiritual perfection of Humanity the stupendous momentum of the
cosmic process has all along been tending.
That spiritual perfection is the true goal of
evolution, the divine end that was involved
in the beginning.   When Huxley asks us to
believe that "the cosmic process has no
sort of relation to moral ends," I feel like
replying with the question, "Does not the
cosmic process exist purely for the sake of
moral ends?"   Subtract from the universe
its ethical meaning, and nothing remains
but an unreal phantom, the figment of false
metaphysics.

We have now arrived at a position from
which a glimmer of light is thrown upon
some of the dark problems connected with
the moral government of the world.   We

can begin to see why misery and wrong-
doing are permitted to exist, and why the
creative energy advances by such slow and
tortuous methods toward the fulfilment of
its divine purpose.   In order to understand
these things, we must ask, What is the
ultimate goal of the ethical process?   According to the utilitarian philosophy that
goal is the completion of human happiness.
But this interpretation soon refutes itself.
A world of completed happiness might well
be a world of quiescence, of stagnation, of
automatism, of blankness; the dynamics of
evolution would have no place in it.   But
suppose we say that the ultimate goal of
the ethical process is the perfecting of human character?   This form of statement
contains far more than the other.   Consummation of happiness is a natural out-
come of the perfecting of character, but
that perfecting can be achieved only through
struggle, through discipline, through resistance.   It is for him that *overcometh* that
the crown of life is reserved.   The con-

summate product of a world of evolution is the character that *creates* happiness, that is replete with dynamic possibilities of fresh life and activity in directions forever new. Such a character is the reflected image of God, and in it are contained the promise and potency of life everlasting.

No such character could be produced by any act of special creation in a garden of Eden. It must be the consummate efflorescence of long ages of evolution, and a world of evolution is necessarily characterized by slow processes, many of which to a looker-on seem like tentative experiments, with an enormous sacrifice of ephemeral forms of life. Thus while the Earth Spirit goes on, unhasting, yet unresting, weaving in the loom of Time the visible garment of God, we begin to see that even what look like failures and blemishes have been from the outset involved in the accomplishment of the all-wise and all-holy purpose, the perfecting of the spiritual Man in the likeness of his Heavenly Father.

These points will receive further indirect illustration as we complete our outline sketch of the cosmic process in the past. It is self-evident that in the production of an ethical character, altruistic feelings and impulses must coöperate. Let us look, then, for some of the beginnings of altruism in the course of the evolution of life.

XI

Maternity and the Evolution of Altruism

ROM an early period of the life-history of our planet, the preservation of the species had obviously become quite as imperative an end as the preservation of individuals; one is at first inclined to say more imperative, but if we pause long enough to remember that total failure to preserve individuals would be equivalent to immediate extinction of the species, we see that the one requirement is as indispensable as the other. Individuals must be preserved, and the struggle for life is between them; species must be preserved, and in the rivalry those have the best chance in which the offspring are either most redundant in numbers or are best cared for. In plants and animals of all but the higher types, the offspring are spores or seeds, larvæ or spawn, or self-maturing eggs. In the absence of parental care the persistence of the species is ensured by the enormous number of such offspring. A single codfish, in a single season, will lay six million eggs, nearly all of which perish, of course, or else in a few years the ocean could not hold all the codfishes. But the princess in the Arabian tale, who fought with the malignant Jinni, could not for her life pick up all the scattered seeds of the pomegranate; and in like manner of the codfish eggs, one in a million or so escapes and the species is maintained. But in the highest types of animal life in birds and mammals — with their four-chambered hearts, completely arterialized blood, and enhanced consciousness — parental care becomes effective in protecting the offspring, and the excessive production diminishes. With birds, the necessity of maintaining a high temperature for the eggs leads to the building of nests, to a division of labour in the securing of food, to the development of

a temporary maternal instinct, and to con-
jugal alliances which in some birds last for
a lifetime. As the eggs become effectively
guarded the number diminishes, till instead
of millions there are half a dozen. When
it comes to her more valuable products,
Nature is not such a reckless squanderer
after all. So with mammals, for the most
part the young are in litters of half a dozen
or so; but in Man, with his prolonged and
costly infancy parental care reaches its
highest development and concentration in
rearing children one by one.

From the dawn of life, I need hardly say,
all the instincts that have contributed to
the preservation of offspring must have
been favoured and cultivated by natural
selection, and in many cases even in types
of life very remote from Humanity, such
instincts have prompted to very different
actions from such as would flow from the
mere instinct of self-preservation. If you
thrust your walking-stick into an ant-heap,
and watch the wild hurry and confusion that

ensues when part of the interior is laid
bare, you will see that all the workers are
busy in moving the larvæ into places of
safety. It is not exactly a maternal instinct, for the workers are not mothers, but
it is an altruistic instinct involving acts of
self-devotion. So in the case of fish that
ascend rivers or bays at spawning time, the
actions of the whole shoal are determined
by a temporarily predominant instinct that
tends towards an altruistic result. In these
and lower grades of life there is already
something at work besides the mere struggle for life between individuals ; there is
something more than mere contention and
slaughter ; there is the effort towards cherishing another life than one's own. In
these regions of animate existence we
catch glimpses of the cosmic roots of love
and self-sacrifice. For the simplest and
rudest productions of Nature mere egoism
might suffice, but to the achievement of
any higher aim some adumbration of altruism was indispensable.

Before such divine things as love and
self-sacrifice could spring up from their
cosmic roots and put forth their efflorescence, it was necessary that conscious personal relations should become established
between mother and infant. We have already observed the critical importance of
these relations in the earliest stages of
the evolution of human society. We may
now add that the relation between mother
and child must have furnished the first
occasion for the sustained and regular development of the altruistic feelings. The
capacity for unselfish devotion called forth
in that relation could afterward be utilized
in the conduct of individuals not thus related to one another.

Of all kinds of altruism the mother's was
no doubt the earliest; it was the derivative
source from which all other kinds were by
slow degrees developed. In the evolution
of these altruistic feelings, therefore, —
feelings which are an absolutely indispensable constituent in the process of ethical

development, — the first appearance of real maternity was an epoch of most profound interest and importance in the history of life upon the earth.

Now maternity, in the true and full sense of the word, is something which was not realized until a comparatively recent stage of the earth's history. God's highest work is never perfected save in the fulness of time. For countless ages there were parents and offspring before the slow but never aimless or wanton cosmic process had brought into existence the conscious personal relationship between mother and child. Protection of eggs and larvæ scarcely suffices for the evolution of true maternity; the relation of moth to caterpillar is certainly very far from being a prototype of it. What spectacle could be more dreary than that of the Jurassic period, with its lords of creation, the oviparous dinosaurs, crawling or bounding over the land, splashing amid the mighty waters, whizzing bat-like through the air, horrible brutes innumerable, with bulky bodies and tiny brains, clumsy, coarse in fibre, and cold-blooded.

" Dragons of the prime,
That tare each other in their slime."

The remnants of that far-off dismal age have been left behind in great abundance, and from them we can easily reconstruct the loathsome picture of a world of dominating egoism, whose redemption through the evolution of true maternity had not yet effectively begun. For such a world might Caliban's theology indeed seem fitted. Nearly nine tenths of our planet's past life-history, measured in duration, had passed away without achieving any higher result than this, — a fact which for impatient reformers may have in it some crumbs of consolation.

For, though the mills of God grind slowly, the cosmic process was aiming at something better than egoism and dinosaurs, and at some time during the long period of the Chalk deposits there began the tremendous world-wide rivalry between these dragons

and the rising class of warm-blooded viviparous mammals which had hitherto played
an insignificant part in the world. The
very name of this class of animals is taken
from the function of motherhood. The offspring of these "mammas" come into the
world as recognizable personalities, so far
developed that the relation between mother
and child begins as a relation of personal
affection. The new-born mammal is not
an egg nor a caterpillar, but a baby, and
the baby's dawning consciousness opens up
a narrow horizon of sympathy and tenderness, a horizon of which the expansion shall
in due course of ages reveal a new heaven
and a new earth. At first the nascent altruism was crude enough, but it must have
sufficed to make mutual understanding and
coöperation more possible than before; it
thus contributed to the advancement of
mammalian intelligence, and prepared the
way for gregariousness, by and by to cul-
minate in sociality, as already described.
In the history of creation the mammals

were moderns, equipped with more effective means of ensuring survival than their
oviparous antagonists. The development of
complete mammality was no sudden thing.
Some of the dinosaurs may have been ovo-
viviparous, like some modern serpents.
The Australian duck-bill, a relic of the
most ancient incipient mammality, is still
oviparous; the opossum and kangaroo preserve the record of a stage when vivipa-
rousness was but partially achieved; but
with the advent of the placental mammals
the break with the old order of things was
complete.

The results of the struggle are registered
in the Eocene rocks. The ancient world
had found its Waterloo. Gone were the
dragons who so long had lorded it over
both hemispheres, — brontosaurs, iguano-
dons, plesiosaurs, lælaps, pterodactyls, —
all gone; their uncouth brood quite vanished from the earth, and nothing left alive
as a reminder, save a few degenerate col-
lateral kin, such as snakes and crocodiles,

objects of dread and loathing to higher creatures. Never in the history of our planet has there been a more sweeping victory than that of the mammals, nor has Nature had any further occasion for victories of that sort. The mammal remains the highest type of animal existence, and subsequent progress has been shown in the perfecting of that type where most perfectible.

XII

The Omnipresent Ethical Trend

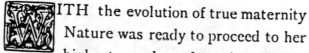

WITH the evolution of true maternity Nature was ready to proceed to her highest grades of work. Intelligence was next to be lifted to higher levels, and the order of mammals with greatest prehensile capacities, the primates with their incipient hands, were the most favourable subjects in which to carry on this process. The later stages of the marvellous story we have already passed in review. We have seen the accumulating intelligence lengthen the period of infancy, and thus prolong the relations of loving sympathy between mother and child; we have seen the human family and human society thus brought into existence; and along therewith we have recognized the necessity laid upon each individual for conforming his conduct to a standard external to himself. At this point, without encountering any breach of continuity in the cosmic process, we crossed the threshold of the ethical world, and entered a region where civilization, or the gradual perfecting of the spiritual qualities, is henceforth Nature's paramount aim. To penetrate further into this region would be to follow the progress of civilization, while the primitive canoe develops into the Cunard steamship, the hieroglyphic battle-sketch into epics and dramas, sun-catcher myths into the Newtonian astronomy, wandering tribes into mighty nations, the ethics of the clan into the moral law for all men. The story shows us Man becoming more and more clearly the image of God, exercising creative attributes, transforming his physical environment, incarnating his thoughts in visible and tangible shapes all over the world, and extorting from the abysses of space the secrets of vanished ages. From lowly beginnings, without breach of continuity, and through the cumulative action of minute and inconspicuous causes, the resistless momentum of cosmic events has tended toward such kind of consummation; and part and parcel of the whole process, inseparably wrapped up with every other part, has been the evolution of the sentiments which tend to subordinate mere egoism to unselfish and moral ends.

A narrow or partial survey might fail to make clear the solidarity of the cosmic process. But the history of creation, when broadly and patiently considered, brings home to us with fresh emphasis the profound truth of what Emerson once said, that "the lesson of life . . . is to believe what the years and the centuries say against the hours; to resist the usurpation of particulars; to penetrate to their catholic sense." When we have learned this lesson, our misgivings vanish, and we breathe a clear atmosphere of faith. Though in many ways God's work is above our comprehension, yet those parts of the world's story that we can decipher well warrant the belief that while in

Nature there may be divine irony, there can
be no such thing as wanton mockery, for
profoundly underlying the surface entangle-
ment of her actions we may discern the
omnipresent ethical trend.   The moral sentiments, the moral law, devotion to unselfish ends, disinterested love, nobility of
soul, — these are Nature's most highly
wrought products, latest in coming to maturity ; they are the consummation, toward
which all earlier prophecy has pointed.
We are right, then, in greeting the rejuve-
nescent summer with devout faith and hope.
Below the surface din and clashing of the
struggle for life we hear the undertone of
the deep ethical purpose, as it rolls in
solemn music through the ages, its volume
swelled by every victory, great or small, of
right over wrong, till in the fulness of time,
in God's own time, it shall burst forth in
the triumphant chorus of Humanity purified
and redeemed.

THE EVERLASTING REALITY
OF RELIGION

———◆———

Here sits he shaping wings to fly;
His heart forebodes a mystery:
He names the name Eternity.

That type of Perfect in his mind
In Nature can he nowhere find,
He sows himself on every wind.

He seems to hear a Heavenly Friend,
And through thick veils to apprehend
A labour working to an end.

TENNYSON, The Two Voices.

I

" Deo erexit Voltaire "

HE visitor to Geneva whose studies have made him duly acquainted with the most interesting human personality of all that are associated with that historic city will never leave the place without making a pilgrimage to the chateau of Ferney. In that refined and quiet rural homestead things still remain very much as on the day when the aged Voltaire left it for the last visit to Paris, where his long life was worthily ended amid words and deeds of affectionate homage. One may sit down at the table where was written the most perfect prose, perhaps, that ever flowed from pen, and look about the little room with its evidences of plain living and high thinking, until one seems to recall the eccentric figure of the vanished Master, with his flashes of shrewd wisdom and caustic wit, his insatiable thirst for knowledge, his consuming hatred of bigotry and oppression, his merciless contempt for shams, his boundless enthusiasm of humanity.   As we stroll in the park, that quaint presence goes along with us till all at once in a shady walk we come upon something highly significant and characteristic, the little parish church with its Latin inscription over the portal, *Deo erexit Voltaire*, i. e. "Voltaire built it for God," and as we muse upon it, the piercing eyes and sardonic but not unkindly smile seem still to follow us.   What meant this eccentric inscription?

When Voltaire became possessor of the manor of Ferney, the church was badly out of repair, and stood where it obstructed the view from certain windows of the chateau. So he had it cleared away, and built in a better spot the new church that is still there.   It was duly consecrated, and the Pope further hallowed it with some relics of ancient saints, and there for many a

year the tenants and dependents of the
manor assembled for divine service. Nowhere in France had Voltaire ever seen a
church dedicated simply to God; it was
always to Our Lady of This or Saint So-
and-so of That; always there was some in-
termediary between the devout soul and the
God of its worship. Not thus should it be
with Voltaire's church, built upon his own
estate to minister to the spiritual needs of
his people. It should be dedicated simply
and without further qualification to the worship and service of God. Furthermore, it
was built and dedicated, not by any ecclesiastical or corporate body, but by the lord of
that manor, the individual layman, Voltaire.

This, I say, was highly characteristic and
significant. It gave terse and pointed expression to Voltaire's way of looking at
such things. Church and theology were
ignored, and the individual soul was left
alone with its God. The Protestant reformers and other freethinkers had stopped
far short of this. In place of an infallible

Church they had left an infallible Book ; if
they rejected transubstantiation, they re-
tained as obligatory such doctrines as those
of the incarnation and atonement ; if they
laughed at the miracles of mediæval saints,
they would allow no discredit to be thrown
upon those of the apostolic age ; in short,
they left standing a large part, if not the
larger part, of the supernatural edifice
within which the religious mind of Europe
had so long been sheltered. But Voltaire
regarded that whole supernatural edifice as
so much rubbish which was impeding the
free development of the human mind, and
ought as quickly as possible to be torn to
pieces and cleared away. His emotions as
well as his reason were concerned in this
conclusion. Organized Christianity, as it
then existed in France, was responsible for
much atrocious injustice, and in neighbour-
ing lands the Inquisition still existed. Ecclesiastical bigotry, the prejudice of ignorance, whatever tended to hold people in
darkness and restrain them from the free

and natural use of their faculties, Voltaire
hated with all the intensity of which he
was capable. He summed it all up in one
abstract term and personified it as " The
Infamous," and the watchword of that life
of tireless vigilance was " Crush the Infamous ! " Supernatural theology had been
too often pressed into the service of " The
Infamous," and for supernatural theology
Voltaire could find no place in his scheme
of things. He lost no chance of assailing
it with mockery and sarcasm made terrible
by the earnestness of his purpose, until he
came in many quarters to be regarded as
the most inveterate antagonist the Church
had ever known.

Yet among the great men of letters in
France contemporary with Voltaire, the
most part went immeasurably farther than
he, and went in a different direction withal,
for they denied the reality of Religion.
Few of them, indeed, believed in the existence of God, or would have had anything
to do with building a house of worship.

It is related of David Hume that when din-
ing once in a party of eighteen at the house
of Baron d'Holbach, he expressed a doubt
as to whether any person could anywhere
be found to avow himself dogmatically an
atheist. " Indeed, my dear sir," quoth the
host, " you are this moment sitting at table
with seventeen such persons." Among
that group of philosophers were men of
great intelligence and lofty purpose, such
as D'Alembert, Diderot, Helvétius, Con-
dorcet, Buffon, men with more of the real
spirit of Christianity in their natures than
could be found in half the churches of
Christendom. The roots of their atheism
were emotional rather than philosophical.
It was part of the generous but rash and
superficial impatience with which they dis-
owned all connection whatever with a
Church that had become subservient to so
much that was bad. Their atheism was
one of the fruits of the vicious policy which
had suppressed Huguenotism in France; it
was an early instance of what has since

been often observed, that materialism and atheism are much more apt to flourish in Romanist than in Protestant countries. The form of religion which is already to some extent purified and rationalized awakens no such violent revulsion in free-thinking minds as the form that is more heavily encumbered with remnants of obsolete primitive thought. Moreover, the rationalizing religion of Protestant countries is commonly found in alliance with political freedom. In France under the Old Régime, the Catholic religion was stigmatized as an ally of despotism, as well as a congeries of absurd doctrines and ceremonies. The best minds felt their common sense shocked by it no less than their reason. No very deep thinking was done on the subject ; their treatment of it was in general extremely shallow.

The forms which religious sentiment had assumed in the Middle Ages had become unintelligible ; the most highly endowed minds were dead to the sublimity of Gothic architecture, and saw nothing but grotesque folly in Dante's poetry. They seriously believed that religious doctrines and ecclesiastical government were originally elaborate systems of fraud, devised by sagacious and crafty tyrants for the sole purpose of enslaving the multitude of mankind. No discrimination was shown. They were as ready to throw away belief in God as in the miracles of St. Columba, and to scout at the notion of a future life in the same terms as those in which they denounced the forged donation of Constantine. The flippant ease with which they disposed of the greatest questions, in crass ignorance of the very nature of the problem to be solved, was well illustrated in the remark of the astronomer Lalande, that he had swept the entire heavens with his telescope and found no God there. A similar instance of missing the point was furnished about fifty years ago by the eminent physiologist Moleschott, when he exclaimed, "No thought without phosphorus," and congratulated himself that

he had forever disposed of the human soul.
I am inclined to think that those are the
two remarks most colossal in their silliness
that ever appeared in print.

Very different in spirit was the acute
reply of Laplace when reminded by Napoleon that his great treatise on the dynamics of the solar system contained no
allusion to God. " Sire," said Laplace, " I
had no need of that hypothesis." This
remark was profound in its truth, for it
meant that in order to give a specific explanation of any single group of phenomena,
it will not do to appeal to divine action,
which is equally the source of all phenomena. Science can deal only with secondary causes. In the eighteenth century
men of science were learning that such is
the case ; men like Diderot and D'Alembert
had come to realize it, and they believed
that the logical result was atheism. This
was because the only idea of God which
they had ever been taught to entertain was
the Latin idea of a God remote from the

world and manifested only through occasional interferences with the order of nature. When they dismissed this idea they declared themselves atheists. If they had been familiar with the Greek idea of God as immanent in the world and manifested at every moment through the orderly sequence of its phenomena, their conclusions would doubtless have been very different.

To these philosophers Voltaire's unshaken theism seemed a mere bit of eccentric conservatism. But along with that queer and intensely independent personality there went a stronger intellectual grasp and a more calm intellectual vision than belonged to any other Frenchman of the eighteenth century. In the facts of Nature, despite the lifeless piecemeal fashion in which they were then studied, Voltaire saw a rational principle at work which atheism could in nowise account for. To him the universe seemed full of evidences of beneficent purpose, and more than once he set forth with eloquence and power the famous argument from design, which is as old as Xenophon's Memorabilia, and which received its fullest development at the hands of Paley and the authors of the Bridgewater Treatises. There is thus yet another significance added to the little church at Ferney. Not only was it the sole church in France dedicated simply to God, and not only was its builder a layman hostile to ecclesiastical doctrines and methods, but he was almost alone among the eminent freethinkers of his age and country in believing in God and asserting the everlasting reality of religion.

It is therefore that I have cited Voltaire as a kind of text for the present discourse; for it is my purpose to show that, apart from all questions of revelation, the light of nature affords us sufficient ground for maintaining that religion is fundamentally true and must endure forever. It appears to me, moreover, that the materialism of the present day is merely a tradition handed down from the French writers whom Vol-

taire combated.   When Moleschott made
his silly remark about phosphorus, it was
simply an inheritance of silliness from Lalande.   When Haeckel tells us that the
doctrine of evolution forbids us to believe
in a future life, it is not because he has
rationally deduced such a conclusion from
the doctrine, but because he takes his opin-
ions on such matters ready-made from Lud-
wig Büchner, who is simply an echo of the
eighteenth century atheist La Mettrie. We
shall see that the doctrine of evolution
has implications very different from what
Haeckel supposes.

But first let me observe in passing that
in the English-speaking world there has
never been any such divorce between ra-
tionalism and religion as in France, and
among the glories of English literature are
such deeply reverent and profoundly philosophical writings as those of Hooker and
Chillingworth, of Bishop Butler and Jona-
than Edwards, and in our own time of Dr.
Martineau.   Nowhere in history, perhaps,

have faith and reason been more harmo-
niously wedded together than in the history of English Protestantism. But the
disturbance that affected France in the age
of Voltaire now affects the whole Christian
world, and every question connected with
religion has been probed to depths of which
the existence was scarcely suspected a century ago. One seldom, indeed, hears the
frivolous mockery in which the old French
writers dealt so freely ; that was an ebulli-
tion of temper called forth by a tyranny
that had come to be a social nuisance.
The scepticism of our day is rather sad
than frivolous ; it drags people from long
cherished notions in spite of themselves ; it
spares but few that are active-minded ; it
invades the church, and does not stop in
the pews to listen but ascends the pulpit
and preaches. There is no refuge anywhere from this doubting and testing spirit
of the age. In the attitude of civilized men
towards the world in which we live, the
change of front has been stupendous ; the

old cosmology has been overthrown in head-
long ruin, attacks upon doctrines have multiplied, and rituals, creeds, and Scriptures
are overhauled and criticised, until a young
generation grows up knowing nothing of
the sturdy faith of its grandfathers save by
hearsay ; for it sees everything in heaven
and earth called upon to show its creden-
tials.

II

The Reign of Law, and the Greek Idea of God

THE general effect of this intellectual movement has been to discredit
more than ever before the Latin
idea of God as a power outside of the course
of nature and occasionally interfering with
it. In all directions the process of evolution has been discovered, working after
similar methods, and this has forced upon
us the belief in the Unity of Nature. We
are thus driven to the Greek conception of
God as the power working in and through
nature, without interference or infraction of
law. The element of chance, which some
atheists formerly admitted into their scheme
of things, is expelled. Nobody would now
waste his time in theorizing about a for-
tuitous concourse of atoms. We have so
far spelled out the history of creation as to

see that all has been done in strict accordance with law. The method has been the
method of evolution, and the more we study
it the more do we discern in it intelligible
coherence. One part of the story never
gives the lie to another part.

So beautiful is all this orderly coherence,
so satisfying to some of our intellectual
needs, that many minds are inclined to
doubt if anything more can be said of the
universe than that it is a Reign of Law,
an endless aggregate of coexistences and
sequences. When we say that one star
attracts another star, we do not really know
that there is any pulling in the case ; all we
know is that a piece of cosmical matter in
the presence of another piece of matter
alters its space-relations in a certain specified way. Among the coexistences and
sequences there is an order which we can
detect, and a few thinkers are inclined to
maintain that this is the whole story. Such
a state of mind, which rests satisfied with
the mere content of observed facts, without

seeking to trace their ultimate implications, is the characteristic of what Auguste Comte called Positivism. It is a more refined phase of atheism than that of the guests at Baron d'Holbach's, but its adherents are few ; for the impetus of modern scientific thought tends with overwhelming force towards the conception of a single First Cause, or Prime Mover, perpetually manifested from moment to moment in all the Protean changes that make up the universe. As I have elsewhere sought to show, this is practically identical with the Athanasian conception of the immanent Deity.[1] Modern men of science often call this view of things Monism, but if questioned narrowly concerning the immanent First Cause, they reply with a general disclaimer of knowledge, and thus entitle themselves to be called by Huxley's term " Agnostics." Thirty-five years ago Spencer, taking a hint from Sir William Hamilton, used the phrase

[1] *The Idea of God as affected by Modern Knowledge,* Boston, 1885.

"The Unknowable" as an equivalent for the immanent Deity considered *per se;* but I always avoid that phrase, for in practice it invariably leads to wrong conceptions, and naturally, since it only expresses one side of the truth. If on the one hand it is impossible for the finite Mind to fathom the Infinite, on the other hand it is practically misleading to apply the term Unknowable to the Deity that is revealed in every pulsation of the wondrously rich and beautiful life of the Universe. For most persons no amount of explanation will prevent the use of the word Unknowable from seeming to remove Deity to an unapproachable distance, whereas the Deity revealed in the process of evolution is the ever-present God without whom not a sparrow falls to the ground, and whose voice is heard in each whisper of conscience, even while his splendour dwells in the white ray from yonder star that began its earthward flight while Abraham's shepherds watched their flocks. It is clear that many persons have

derived from Spencer's use of the word
Unknowable an impression that he intends
by means of metaphysics to refine God
away into nothing; whereas he no more
cherishes any such intention than did St.
Paul, when he asked, "Who hath known
the mind of the Lord, or who hath been his
counsellor?"—no more than Isaiah did
when he declared that even as the heavens
are higher than the earth, so are Jehovah's
ways higher than our ways and his thoughts
than our thoughts.

III

Weakness of Materialism

UST here comes along the materialist and asks us some questions, tries to serve on us a kind of metaphysical writ of *quo warranto*. If modern physics leads us inevitably to the conception of a single infinite Power manifested in all the phenomena of the knowable Universe, by what authority do we identify that Power with the indwelling Deity as conceived by St. Athanasius? The Athanasian Deity is to some extent fashioned in Man's image; he is, to say the least, like the psychical part of ourselves. After making all possible allowances for the gulf which separates that which is Infinite and Absolute from that which is Finite and Relative, an essential kinship is asserted between God and the Human Soul. By what authority, our materialist will ask, do we assert any such kinship between the Human Soul and the Power which modern physics reveals as active throughout the universe? Is it not going far beyond our knowledge to assert any such kinship? And would it not be more modest and becoming in us to simply designate this ever active universal Power by some purely scientific term, such as Force?

This argument is to-day a very familiar one, and it wears a plausible aspect; it is couched in a spirit of scientific reserve, which wins for it respectful consideration. The modest and cautious spirit of science has done so much for us, that it is always wise to give due heed to its warnings. Let us beware of going beyond our knowledge, says the materialist. We know nothing but phenomena as manifestations of an indwelling force; nor have we any ground for supposing that there is anything psychical, or even quasi-psychical, in the universe outside of the individual minds of men and other animals.   Moreover, continues the materialist, the psychical phenomena of which we are conscious — reason, memory, emotion, volition — are but peculiarly conditioned manifestations of the same indwelling force which under other conditions appears as light or heat or electricity.   All such manifestations are fleeting, and beyond this world of fleeting phenomena we have no warrant, either in science or in common sense, for supposing that anything whatever exists.   This world that is cognizable through the senses is all that there is, and the story of it that we can decipher by the aid of terrestrial experience is the whole story; the Unseen World is a mere figment inherited from the untutored fancy of primeval man.   Such is the general view of things which Materialism urges upon us with the plea of scientific sobriety and caution; and to many minds, as already observed, it wears a plausible aspect.

Nevertheless, when subjected to criticism, this theory of things soon loses its

sober and plausible appearance and is seen
to be eminently rash and shallow. In the
first place, there is no such correlation or
equivalence as is alleged between physical
forces and the phenomena of consciousness.
The correlations between different modes
of motion have been proved by actual quan-
titative measurement, and never could have
been proved in any other way. We know,
for example, that heat is a mode of motion;
the heat that will raise the temperature of
a pound of water by one degree of Fahren-
heit is exactly equivalent to the motion of
772 pounds falling through a distance of
one foot. In similar wise we know that
light, electricity, and magnetism are modes
of motion, transferable one into another;
and, although precise measurements have
not been accomplished, there is no reason
for doubting that the changes in brain tissue, which accompany each thought and
feeling, are also modes of motion, transferable into the other physical modes. But
thought and feeling themselves, which can

neither be weighed nor measured, do not admit of being resolved into modes of motion. They do not enter into the closed circuit of physical transformations, but stand forever outside of it, and concentric with that segment of the circuit which passes through the brain. It may be that thought and feeling could not continue to exist if that physical segment of the circuit were taken away. It may be that they could. To assume that they could not is surely the height of rash presumption. The correlation of forces exhibits Mind as in nowise a product of Matter, but as something in its growth and manifestations outside and parallel. It is incompatible with the theory that the relation of the human soul to the body is like that of music to the harp; but it is quite compatible with the time-honoured theory of the human soul as indwelling in the body and escaping from it at death.

In the second place, when we come to the denial of all kinship between the hu-

man soul and the Infinite Power that is
revealed in all phenomena, the materialistic
theory raises difficulties as great as those
which it seeks to avoid. The difficulties
which it wishes to avoid are those which inevitably encumber the attempt to conceive
of Deity as Personality exerting volition
and cherishing intelligent purpose. Such
difficulties are undeniably great ; nay, they
are insuperable. When we speak of Intelligence and Will and Personality, we must
use these words with the meanings in which
experience has clothed them, or we shall
soon find ourselves talking nonsense. The
only intelligence we know is strictly serial
in its nature, and is limited by the existence of independent objects of cognition.
What flight of analogy can bear us across
the gulf that divides such finite intelligence
from that unlimited Knowledge to which
all things past and future are ever present ?
Volition, as we know it, implies alternative
courses of action, antecedent motives, and
resulting effort. Like intelligence, its op-

erations are serial. What, then, do we really mean, if we speak of omnipresent Volition achieving at one and the same moment an infinite variety of ends? So, too, with Personality: when we speak of personality that is not circumscribed by limits, are we not using language from which all the meaning has evaporated?

Such difficulties are insurmountable. Words which have gained their meanings from finite experience of finite objects of thought must inevitably falter and fail when we seek to apply them to that which is Infinite. But we do not mend matters by emp'oying terms taken from the inorganic world rather than from human personality. To designate the universal Power by some scientific term, such as Force, does not help us in the least. All our experience of force is an experience of finite forces antagonized by other forces. We can frame no conception whatever of Infinite Force comprising within itself all the myriad antagonistic attractions and repulsions in which the dynamic universe consists. We go beyond our knowledge when we speak of Infinite Force quite as much as we do when we speak of Infinite Personality. Indeed, no word or phrase which we seek to apply to Deity can be other than an extremely inadequate and unsatisfactory symbol. From the very nature of the case it must always be so, and if we once understand the reason why, it need not vex or puzzle us.

It is not only when we try to speculate about Deity that we find ourselves encompassed with difficulties and are made to realize how very short is our mental tether in some directions. This world, in its commonest aspects, presents many baffling problems, of which it is sometimes wholesome that we should be reminded. If you look at a piece of iron, it seems solid; it looks as if its particles must be everywhere in contact with one another. And yet, by hammering, or by great pressure, or by intense cold, the piece of iron may be compressed, so that it will occupy less space than before. Evidently, then, its particles are not in contact, but are separated from one another by unoccupied tracts of enveloping space. In point of fact, these particles are atoms arranged after a complicated fashion in clusters known as molecules. The word *atom* means something that cannot be cut. Now, are these iron atoms divisible or indivisible? If they are divisible, then what of the parts into which each one can be divided; are they also divisible? and so on forever. But if these iron atoms are indivisible, how can we conceive such a thing? Can we imagine two sides so close together that no plane of cleavage could pass between them? Can we imagine cohesive tenacity too great to be overcome by any assignable disruptive force, and therefore infinite? Suppose, now, we heat this piece of iron to a white heat. Scientific inquiry has revealed the fact that its atom-clusters are floating in an ocean of ether, in which are also floating the atom-clusters of other bodies and of the air about us. The heating is the increase of wave motion in this ether, until presently a secondary series of intensely rapid waves appear as white light. Now this ether would seem to be of infinite rarity, since it does not affect the weight of bodies, and yet its wave-motions imply an elasticity far greater than that of coiled steel. How can we imagine such powerful resilience combined with such extreme tenuity?

These are a few of the difficulties of conception in which the study of physical science abounds, and I cite them because it is wholesome for us to bear in mind that such difficulties are not confined to theological subjects. They serve to show how our powers of conceiving ideas are strictly limited by the nature of our experience. The illustration just cited from the luminiferous ether simply shows how during the past century the study of radiant forces has introduced us to a mode of material existence quite different from anything that had formerly been known or suspected. In this mode of matter we find attributes united which all previous experience had taught us to regard as contradictory and incompatible. Yet the facts cannot be denied; hard as we may find it to frame the conception, this light-bearing substance is at the same time almost infinitely rare and almost infinitely resilient. If such difficulties confront us upon the occasion of a fresh extension of our knowledge of the physical world, what must we expect when we come to speculate upon the nature and modes of existence of God? Bearing this in mind, let us proceed to consider the assumption that the Infinite Power which is manifested in the universe is essentially psychical in its nature; in other words, that between God and the Human Soul there is real kinship, although we may be unable to render any scientific account of it. Let us consider this assumption historically, and in the light of our general knowledge of Evolution.

IV

Religion's First Postulate : the Quasi-Human God

T is with purpose that I use the word *assumption*. As a matter of history, the existence of a quasi-human God has always been an assumption or postulate. It is something which men have all along taken for granted. It probably never occurred to anybody to try to prove the existence of such a God until it was doubted, and doubts on that subject are very modern. Omitting from the account a few score of ingenious philosophers, it may be said that all mankind, the wisest and the simplest, have taken for granted the existence of a Deity, or deities, of a psychical nature more or less similar to that of Humanity. Such a postulate has formed a part of all human thinking from primitive ages down to the present time. The forms in which it has appeared have been myriad in number, but all have been included in this same fundamental assumption. The earliest forms were those which we call fetishism and animism. In fetishism the wind that blows a tree down is endowed with personality and supposed to exert conscious effort; in animism some ghost of a dead man is animating that gust of wind. In either case a conscious volition similar to our own, but outside of us, is supposed to be at work. There has been some discussion as to whether fetishism or animism is the more primitive, and some writers would regard fetishism as a special case of animism; but it is not necessary to my present purpose that such questions should be settled. The main point is this, that in the earliest phases of theism each operation of Nature was supposed to have some quasi-human personality behind it. Such phases we find among contemporary savages, and there is abundant evidence of

their former existence among peoples now
civilized. In the course of ages there was
a good deal of generalizing done. Poseidon
could shake the land and preside over the
sea, angry Apollo could shoot arrows tipped
with pestilence, mischievous Hermes could
play pranks in the summer breezes, while
as lord over all, though with somewhat fitful
sway, stood Zeus on the summit of Olympus, gathering the rain-clouds and wielding
the thunderbolt. Nothing but increasing
knowledge of nature was needed to convert
such Polytheism into Monotheism, even into
the strict Monotheism of our own time, in
which the whole universe is the multiform
manifestation of a single Deity that is still
regarded as in some real and true sense
quasi-human. As the notion of Deity has
thus been gradually generalized, from a
thousand local gods to one omnipresent
God, it has been gradually stripped of its
grosser anthropomorphic vestments. The
tutelar Deity of a savage clan is supposed
to share with his devout worshippers in the

cannibal banquet; the Gods of Olympus made war and love, and were moved to fits of inextinguishable laughter. From our modern Monotheism such accidents of humanity are eliminated, but the notion of a kinship between God and man remains, and is rightly felt to be essential to theism. Take away from our notion of God the human element, and the theism instantly vanishes; it ceases to be a notion of God. We may retain an abstract symbol to which we apply some such epithet as Force, or Energy, or Power, but there is nothing theistic in this. Some ingenious philosopher may try to persuade us to the contrary, but the Human Soul knows better; it knows at least what it wants; it has asked for Theology, not for Dynamics, and it resents all such attempts to palm off upon it stones for bread.

Our philosopher will here perhaps lift up his hands in dismay and cry, " Hold! what matters it what the Human Soul wants? Are cravings, forsooth, to be made to do duty as reasons?" It is proper to reply that we are trying to deal with this whole subject after the manner of the naturalist, which is to describe things as they exist and account for them as best we may. I say, then, that mankind have framed, and for long ages maintained, a notion of God into which there enters a human element. Now if it should ever be possible to abolish that human element, it would not be possible to cheat mankind into accepting the non-human remnant of the notion as an equivalent of the full notion of which they had been deprived. Take away from our symbolic conception of God the human element, and that aspect of theism which has from the outset chiefly interested mankind is gone.

V

Religion's Second Postulate : the undying Human Soul

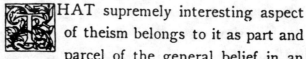HAT supremely interesting aspect of theism belongs to it as part and parcel of the general belief in an Unseen World, in which human beings have an interest. The belief in the personal continuance of the individual human soul after death is a very ancient one. The savage custom of burying utensils and trinkets for the use of the deceased enables us to trace it back into the Glacial Period. We may safely say that for much more than a hundred thousand years mankind have regarded themselves as personally interested in two worlds, the physical world which daily greets our waking senses, and another world, comparatively dim and vaguely outlined, with which the psychical

side of humanity is more closely connected. The belief in the Unseen World seems to be coextensive with theism ; the animism of the lowest savages includes both. No race or tribe of men has ever been found destitute of the belief in a ghost-world. Now, a ghost-world implies the personal continuance of human beings after death, and it also implies identity of nature between the ghosts of man and the indwelling spirits of sun, wind, and flood. It is chiefly because these ideas are so closely interwoven in savage thought that it is often so difficult to discriminate between fetishism and animism. These savage ideas are of course extremely crude in their symbolism. With the gradual civilization of human thinking, the refinement in the conception of the Deity is paralleled by the refinement in the conception of the Other World. From Valhalla to Dante's Paradise, what an immeasurable distance the human mind has travelled ! In our modern Monotheism the assumption of kinship be-

tween God and the Human Soul is the assumption that there is in Man a psychical
element identical in nature with that which
is eternal. Belief in a quasi-human God
and belief in the Soul's immortality thus
appear in their origin and development, as
in their ultimate significance, to be inseparably connected. They are part and parcel
of one and the same efflorescence of the
human mind. Mankind has always entertained them in common, and so entertains
them now; and were it possible (which it
is not) for science to disprove the Soul's
immortality, a theism deprived of this element would surely never be accepted as
an equivalent for the theism entertained
before. The Positivist argument that the
only worthy immortality is survival in the
grateful remembrance of one's fellow creatures would hardly be regarded as anything
but a travesty and trick. If the world's
long cherished beliefs are to fall, in God's
name let them fall, but save us from the
intellectual hypocrisy that goes about pretending we are none the poorer!

VI

Religion's Third Postulate : the Ethical Significance of the Unseen World

OUR account of the rise and progress of the general belief in an Unseen World is, however, not yet complete. No mention has been made of an element which apparently has always been present in the belief. I mean the ethical element. The savage's primeval ghost-world is always mixed up with his childlike notions of what he ought to do and what he ought not to do. The native of Tierra del Fuego, who foreboded a snowstorm because one of Mr. Darwin's party killed some birds for specimens, furnishes an excellent illustration. In a tribe living always on the brink of starvation, any wanton sacrifice of meat must awaken the wrath of the tutelar ancestral ghost-deities

who control the weather. Notions of a similar sort are connected with the direful host
of omens that dog the savage's footsteps
through the world. Whatever conduct the
necessities of clan or tribe have prohibited
soon comes to wear the aspect of sacrilege.

Thus inextricably intertwined from the
moment of their first dim dawning upon the
consciousness of nascent Humanity, have
been the notion of Deity, the notion of an
Unseen World, and the notions of Right
and Wrong. In their beginnings theology
and ethics were inseparable; in all the vast
historic development of religion they have
remained inseparable. The grotesque conceptions of primitive men have given place
to conceptions framed after wider and
deeper experience, but the union of ethics
with theology remains undisturbed even
in that most refined religious philosophy
which ventures no opinion concerning the
happiness or misery of a future life, except
that the seed sown here will naturally de-
termine the fruit to be gathered hereafter.

All the analogies that modern knowledge
can bring to bear upon the theory of a
future life point to the opinion that the
breach of physical continuity is not accom-
panied by any breach of ethical continuity.
Such an opinion relating to matters beyond experience cannot of course be called
scientific, but whether it be justifiable or
not, my point is that neither in the crude
fancies of primitive men nor in the most
refined modern philosophy can theology
divorce itself from ethics. Take away the
ethical significance from our conceptions of
the Unseen World and the quasi-human
God, and no element of significance remains. All that was vital in theism is
gone.

VII

Is the Substance of Religion a Phantom, or an Eternal Reality ?

E are now prepared to see what is involved in the Reality of Religion. Speaking historically, it may be said that Religion has always had two sides : on the one side it has consisted of a theory, more or less elaborate, and on the other side it has consisted of a group of sentiments conformable to the theory. Now in all ages and in every form of Religion, the theory has comprised three essential elements : first, belief in Deity, as quasi-human ; secondly, belief in an Unseen World in which human beings continue to exist after death ; thirdly, recognition of the ethical aspects of human life as related in a special and intimate sense to this Unseen World. These three elements are alike indispensable. If any one of the three be taken away, the remnant cannot properly be called Religion. Is then the subject-matter of Religion something real and substantial, or is it a mere figment of the imagination? Has Religion through all these weary centuries been dealing with an eternal verity, or has it been blindly groping after a phantom? Can that history of the universe which we call the Doctrine of Evolution be made to furnish any lesson that will prove helpful in answering this question? We shall find, I think, that it does furnish such a lesson.

But first let us remember that along with the three indispensable elements here specified, every historic Religion has also contained a quantity of cosmological speculations, metaphysical doctrines, priestly rites and ceremonies and injunctions, and a very considerable part of this structure has been demolished by modern criticism. The destruction of beliefs has been so great that we can hardly think it strange if some critics have taken it into their heads that nothing can be rescued. But let us see what the doctrine of evolution has to say. Our inquiry may seem to take us very far afield, but that we need not mind if we find the answer by and by directing us homeward.

VIII

The Fundamental Aspect of Life

 OFTEN think, when working over my plants, of what Linnæus once said of the unfolding of a blossom: "I saw God in His glory passing near me, and bowed my head in worship." The scientific aspect of the same thought has been put into words by Tennyson: —

> " Flower in the crannied wall,
>   I pluck you out of the crannies,
>   I hold you here, root and all, in my hand,
>   Little flower, — but if I could understand
>   What you are, root and all, and all in all,
>   I should know what God and man is."

No deeper thought was ever uttered by poet. For in this world of plants, which with its magician chlorophyll conjuring with sunbeams is ceaselessly at work bringing life out of death, — in this quiet vegetable world we may find the elementary

principles of all life in almost visible operation. It is one of these elementary principles — a very simple and broad one — that
here concerns us.

One of the greatest contributions ever
made to scientific knowledge is Herbert
Spencer's profound and luminous exposi-
tion of Life as the continuous adjustment
of inner relations to outer relations. The
extreme simplicity of the subject in its
earliest illustrations is such that the stu-
dent at first hardly suspects the wealth of
knowledge toward which it is pointing the
way. The most fundamental characteristic
of living things is their response to external
stimuli. If you come upon a dog lying by
the roadside and are in doubt whether he
is alive or dead, you poke him with a stick ;
if you get no response you presently conclude that it is a dead dog. So if the tree
fails to put forth leaves in response to the
rising vernal temperature, it is an indication
of death. Pour water on a drooping plant,
and it shows its life by rearing its head.

The growth of a plant is in its ultimate analysis a group of motions put forth in adjustment to a group of physical and chemical conditions in the soil and atmosphere. A fine illustration is the spiral distribution of leaves about the stem, at different angular intervals in different kinds of plants, but always so arranged as to ensure the most complete exposure of the chlorophyll to the sunbeams. Every feature of the plant is explicable on similar principles. It is the result of a continuous adjustment of relations within the plant to relations existing outside of it. It is important that we should form a clear conception of this, and a contrasted instance will help us. Take one of those storm-glasses in which the approach of atmospheric disturbance sets up a feathery crystallization that changes in shape and distribution as the state of the air outside changes. Here is something that simulates vegetable life, but there is a profound difference. In every one of these changes the liquid in the storm-glass is passive; it is changed and waits until it is changed again. But in the case of a tree, when the increased supply of solar radiance in spring causes those internal motions which result in the putting forth of leaves, it is quite another affair. Here the external change sets. up an internal change which leads to a second internal change that anticipates a second external change. It is this active response that is the mark of life.

All life upon the globe, whether physical or psychical, represents the continuous adjustment of inner to outer relations. The degree of life is low or high, according as the correspondence between internal and external relations is simple or complex, limited or extensive, partial or complete, perfect or imperfect. The relations established within a plant answer only to the presence or absence of a certain quantity of light and heat, and to sundry chemical and physical relations in atmosphere and soil. In a polyp, besides general relations

similar to these, certain more special relations are established in correspondence
with the eternal existence of mechanical
irritants ; as when its tentacles contract on
being touched. The increase of extension
acquired by the correspondences as we
ascend the animal scale may be seen by
contrasting the polyp, which can simply
distinguish between soluble and insoluble
matter, or between opacity and translucence in its environment, with the keen-
scented bloodhound and the far-sighted
vulture. And the increase of complexity
may be appreciated by comparing the motions respectively gone through by the
polyp on the one hand, and by the dog and
vulture on the other, while securing and
disposing of their prey. The more specific
and accurate, the more complex and extensive, is the response to environing relations,
the higher and richer, we say, is the life.

IX

How the Evolution of Senses expands the World

HE whole progression of life upon the globe, in so far as it has been achieved through natural selection, has consisted in the preservation and the propagation of those living creatures in whom the adjustment of inner relations to outer relations is most successful. This is only a more detailed and descriptive way of saying that natural selection is equivalent to survival of the fittest. The shapes of animals, as well as their capacities, have been evolved through almost infinitely slow increments of adjustment upon adjustment. In this way, for instance, has been evolved the vertebrate skeleton, through a process of which Spencer's wonderful analysis is as thrilling as a poem. Or consider the development of the special organs of sense. Among the most startling disclosures of embryology are those which relate to this subject. The most perfect organs of touch are the *vibrissæ* or whiskers of the cat, which act as long levers in communicating impulses to the nerve-fibres that terminate in clusters about the dermal sacs in which they are inserted. These cat-whiskers are merely specialized forms of such hairs as those which cover the bodies of most mammals, and which remain in evanescent shape upon the human skin imbedded in minute sacs. Now in their origin the eye and ear are identical with *vibrissæ*. In the early stages of vertebrate life, while the differentiations of dermal tissue went mostly to the production of hairs or feathers or scales, sundry special differentiations went to the production of ears and eyes. Embryology shows that in mammals the bulb of the eye and the auditory chamber are extremely metamorphosed hair-sacs, the crystalline lens is a differentiated hair, and the aqueous and vitreous humours are liquefied dermal tissue! The implication of these wonderful facts is that sight and hearing were slowly differentiated from the sense of touch. One can seem to discern how in the history of the eye there was at first a concentration of pigment grains in a particular dermal sac, making that spot exceptionally sensitive to light; then came by slow degrees the heightened translucence, the convexity of surface, the refracting humours, and the multiplication of nerve-vesicles arranging themselves as retinal rods. And what was the result of all this for the creature in whom organs of vision were thus developed? There was an immense extension of the range, complexity, and definiteness of the adjustment of inner relations to outer relations ; in other words, there was an immense increase of life. There came into existence, moreover, for those with eyes to see it, a mighty visible world that for sightless creatures had been virtually non-existent.

With the further progress of organic life, the high development of the senses was attended or followed by increase of brain development and the correlative intelligence, immeasurably enlarging the scope of the correspondences between the living creature and the outer world.   In the case of Man, the adjustments by which we meet the exigencies of life from day to day are largely psychical, achieved by the aid of ideal representations of environing circumstances.   Our actions are guided by our theory of the situation, and it needs no illustration to show us that a true theory is an adjustment of one's ideas to the external facts, and that such adjustments are helps to successful living.   The whole worth of education is directed toward cultivating the capacity of framing associations of ideas that conform to objective facts.   It is thus that life is guided.

X

Nature's Eternal Lesson is the Everlasting
Reality of Religion

O as we look back over the marvellous life-history of our planet, even
from the dull time when there was
no life more exalted than that of conferva
scum on the surface of a pool, through
ages innumerable until the present time
when Man is learning how to decipher Nature's secrets, we look back over an infinitely slow series of minute adjustments,
gradually and laboriously increasing the
points of contact between the inner Life
and the World environing. Step by step
in the upward advance toward Humanity
the environment has enlarged. The world
of the fresh-water alga was its tiny pool
during its brief term of existence; the
world of civilized man comprehends the

stellar universe during countless æons of
time.   Every stage of enlargement has had
reference to actual existences outside.   The
eye was developed in response to the outward existence of radiant light, the ear in
response to the outward existence of acous-
tic vibrations, the mother's love came in
response to the infant's needs, fidelity and
honour were slowly developed as the nascent social life required them ; everywhere
the internal adjustment has been brought
about so as to harmonize with some actually
existing external fact.   Such has been Nature's method, such is the deepest law of
life that science has been able to detect.

Now there was a critical moment in the
history of our planet, when love was beginning to play a part hitherto unknown, when
notions of right and wrong were germinat-
ing in the nascent Human Soul, when the
family was coming into existence, when
social ties were beginning to be knit, when
winged words first took their flight through
the air.   It was the moment when the pro-

cess of evolution was being shifted to a
higher plane, when civilization was to be
superadded to organic evolution, when the
last and highest of creatures was coming
upon the scene, when the dramatic purpose
of creation was approaching fulfilment.
At that critical moment we see the nascent
Human Soul vaguely reaching forth toward
something akin to itself not in the realm
of fleeting phenomena but in the Eternal
Presence beyond. An internal adjustment
of ideas was achieved in correspondence
with an Unseen World. That the ideas
were very crude and childlike, that they
were put together with all manner of gro-
tesqueness, is what might be expected.
The cardinal fact is that the crude childlike mind was groping to put itself into
relation with an ethical world not visible to
the senses. And one aspect of this fact,
not to be lightly passed over, is the fact
that Religion, thus ushered upon the scene
coeval with the birth of Humanity, has
played such a dominant part in the subse-

quent evolution of human society that what
history would be without it is quite beyond
imagination.   As to the dimensions of this
cardinal fact there can thus be no question.
None can deny that it is the largest and
most ubiquitous fact connected with the
existence of mankind upon the earth.

Now if the relation thus established in
the morning twilight of Man's existence
between the Human Soul and a world invisible and immaterial is a relation of which
only the subjective term is real and the objective term is non-existent, then, I say, it
is something utterly without precedent in
the whole history of creation.   All the analogies of Evolution, so far as we have yet
been able to decipher it, are overwhelming
against any such supposition.   To suppose
that during countless ages, from the sea-
weed up to Man, the progress of life was
achieved through adjustments to external
realities, but that then the method was all
at once changed and throughout a vast
province of evolution the end was secured

through adjustments to external non-reali-
ties, is to do sheer violence to logic and to
common sense. Or, to vary the form of
statement, since every adjustment whereby
any creature sustains life may be called a
true step, and every maladjustment whereby
life is wrecked may be called a false step;
if we are asked to believe that Nature, after
having throughout the whole round of her
inferior products achieved results through
the accumulation of all true steps and pitiless rejection of all false steps, suddenly
changed her method and in the case of
her highest product began achieving results
through the accumulation of false steps; I
say we are entitled to resent such a suggestion as an insult to our understandings.
All the analogies of Nature fairly shout
against the assumption of such a breach of
continuity between the evolution of Man
and all previous evolution. So far as our
knowledge of Nature goes the whole momentum of it carries us onward to the
conclusion that the Unseen World, as the

objective term in a relation of fundamental importance that has coexisted with the whole career of Mankind, has a real existence; and it is but following out the analogy to regard that Unseen World as the theatre where the ethical process is destined to reach its full consummation. The lesson of evolution is that through all these weary ages the Human Soul has not been cherishing in Religion a delusive phantom, but in spite of seemingly endless groping and stumbling it has been rising to the recognition of its essential kinship with the ever-living God. Of all the implications of the doctrine of evolution with regard to Man, I believe the very deepest and strongest to be that which asserts the Everlasting Reality of Religion.

So far as I am aware, the foregoing argument is here advanced for the first time. It does not pretend to meet the requirements of scientific demonstration. One must not look for scientific demonstration in problems that contain so many factors tran-

scending our direct experience.   But as an
appeal to our common sense, the argument
here brought forward surely has tremendous weight.   It seems to me far more
convincing than any chain of subtle metaphysical reasoning can ever be ; for such
chains, however, invincible in appearance,
are no stronger than the weakest of their
links, and in metaphysics one is always un-
easily suspecting some undetected flaw.
My argument represents the impression
that is irresistibly forced upon one by a
broad general familiarity with Nature's processes and methods ; it therefore belongs
to the class of arguments that survive.

Observe, too, that it is far from being a
modified repetition of the old argument
that beliefs universally accepted must be
true.   Upon the view here presented, every
specific opinion ever entertained by man
respecting religious things may be wrong,
and in all probability is exceedingly crude,
and yet the Everlasting Reality of Religion, in its three indispensable elements as

here set forth, remains unassailable. Our common-sense argument puts the scientific presumption entirely and decisively on the side of religion and against all atheistic and materialistic explanations of the universe. It establishes harmony between our highest knowledge and our highest aspirations by showing that the latter no less than the former are a normal result of the universal cosmic process. It has nothing to fear from the advance of scientific discovery, for as these things .come to be better understood, it is going to be realized that the days of the antagonism between Science and Religion must by and by come to an end. That antagonism has been chiefly due to the fact that religious ideas were until lately allied with the doctrine of special creations. They have therefore needed to be remodelled and considered from new points of view. But we have at length reached a stage where it is becoming daily more and more apparent that with the deeper study of Nature the old strife between faith and knowledge is drawing to a close ; and disentangled at last from that ancient slough of despond the Human Mind will breathe a freer air and enjoy a vastly extended horizon.

L'ENVOI

———◆———

Yesterday, when weary with writing, and my mind quite dusty with considering these atoms, I was called to supper, and a salad I had asked for was set before me. "It seems, then," said I aloud, "that if pewter dishes, leaves of lettuce, grains of salt, drops of vinegar and oil, and slices of eggs, had been floating about in the air from all eternity, it might at last happen by chance that there would come a salad." "Yes," says my wife, "but not so nice and well-dressed as this of mine is!" — KEPLER, *apud* Tait and Stewart, *Paradoxical Philosophy*.